# TAKING ON THE B.E.S.T

# 5TH GRADE MATH

## STUDENT WORKBOOK

IT'S A GOOD DAY TO DO MATH

A high-energy math program aligned specifically to Florida's B.E.S.T. Standards for Math

Video Lessons with Ms. McCarthy

Extra Practice to Promote Student Growth

Math Tasks, Error Analysis & More

Created by Sarah McCarthy

# HEY WORLD CHANGER!

I just wanted to take a moment to introduce myself. My name is Ms. McCarthy, and I am so excited to be a part of your math journey this year. My mission is to make math FUN, make it CLICK, and make it STICK for you. I will be there to support you by walking you through the skills and tools you will need to be successful in math this year, but that will only take you so far.

You see, your willingness to try and persistence to keep going even when it gets tough will be the keys to your success . I challenge you to take charge of your learning and stick with each math skill until you get it. Think you can handle that? I believe in you and know that you can do this!

Go ahead and commit to learning and growing this year by filling out the statement below:

I, _____, hereby make a sincere commitment to give this school year everything I've got. I will take charge of my learning by asking questions and solving problems to the best of my ability. When work is challenging for me, I will stay determined and stick with it until I get it.

Sign your name: X _____

Way to go! Let's get to it, and "LET ME TEACH YA!"

*— Ms. McCarthy*

# "TAKING ON THE B.E.S.T."
## Theme Song

Do you know what the BEST version of you looks like?
Just take a look in the mirror,
The person that you were born to be and say,
"I'M TAKING ON THE BEST!"

Every day is a new day to step it up
And maybe some days I feel like giving up
I just don't get it,
but I can't forget
That I'm a believer in the POWER OF YET!

I may not know it now, but I will
Take a deep breath, and I'm chill
Mistakes are part of the game,
I embrace 'em
I don't run from my fears,
I face 'em

How?
I pay attention
I take charge of my learning
Draw it out, and work it out
To show my journey
Try until it clicks,
Make sure that it sticks,
Working at it constantly is my secret

Practice is not something I do once I'm good
It's the one thing I do that makes me good
So I take another step
I'm obsessed with progress
You know why? (Why?)
I'M TAKING ON THE BEST!

# MATHEMATICAL
## Mindset Creed

**THIS IS A SAFE PLACE TO MAKE MISTAKES.**
Mistakes help me learn and grow.

**I AM A HARD WORKER.**
I stick with it until I get it.

**I AM BRAVE. I TAKE CHARGE OF MY LEARNING.**
I ask questions when I don't understand.

**WHEN IN DOUBT, I DRAW IT OUT (IF POSSIBLE).**
And it's always possible to work it out.

**I RESPECT AND ACTIVELY LISTEN**
To the ideas of others.

## NOTES

_____

_____

_____

_____

_____

_____

_____

# TABLE OF CONTENTS

(MA.5.NSO.1.3 continues on next page)

*Video lessons can only be viewed with a membership at McCarthyMathAcademy.com*

# TABLE OF CONTENTS

*Video lessons can only be viewed with a membership at McCarthyMathAcademy.com*

# TABLE OF CONTENTS

# TABLE OF CONTENTS

*Video lessons can only be viewed with a membership at McCarthyMathAcademy.com*

# TABLE OF CONTENTS

# TABLE OF CONTENTS

*Video lessons can only be viewed with a membership at McCarthyMathAcademy.com*

# TABLE OF CONTENTS

# TABLE OF CONTENTS

*Video lessons can only be viewed with a membership at McCarthyMathAcademy.com*

# TABLE OF CONTENTS

# TABLE OF CONTENTS

*Video lessons can only be viewed with a membership at McCarthyMathAcademy.com*

# TABLE OF CONTENTS

(MA.5.GR.1.1 continues on next page)

*Video lessons can only be viewed with a membership at McCarthyMathAcademy.com*

# TABLE OF CONTENTS

(MA.5.GR.2.1 continues on next page)

*Video lessons can only be viewed with a membership at McCarthyMathAcademy.com*

# TABLE OF CONTENTS

*Video lessons can only be viewed with a membership at McCarthyMathAcademy.com*

# TABLE OF CONTENTS

*Video lessons can only be viewed with a membership at McCarthyMathAcademy.com*

# TABLE OF CONTENTS

(MA.5.DP.1.2 continues on next page)

*Video lessons can only be viewed with a membership at McCarthyMathAcademy.com*

# TABLE OF CONTENTS

 Video Lesson **Foundational Skills**

### PLACE VALUE

| 2 | 1 | 9 | . | 3 | 0 | 8 |
|---|---|---|---|---|---|---|

### VALUE OF DIGITS

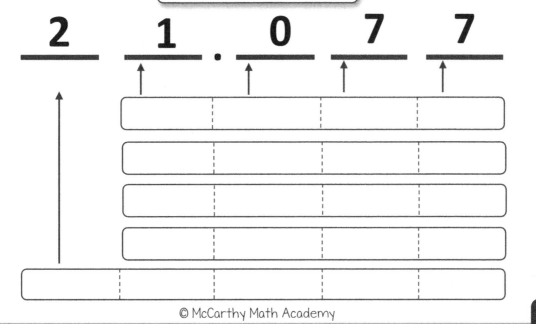

| 2 | 1 | . | 0 | 7 | 7 |
|---|---|---|---|---|---|

# TAKING ON THE B.E.S.T.

  Video Lesson | **10 Times Greater/Less**

**1** Write the number 47.51 in the place value chart below.

| Hundreds | Tens | Ones | Tenths | Hundredths | Thousandths |
|----------|------|------|--------|------------|-------------|
|          |      |      |        |            |             |

| Write a number that is ten times greater than 47.51. | |
|---|---|
| Write a number that is ten times less, or one–tenth of 47.51. | |

**2** Write the number 9.02 in the place value chart below.

| Hundreds | Tens | Ones | Tenths | Hundredths | Thousandths |
|----------|------|------|--------|------------|-------------|
|          |      |      |        |            |             |

| Write a number that is ten times greater than 9.02. | |
|---|---|
| Write a number that is ten times less, or one–tenth of 9.02. | |

21

# TAKING ON THE B.E.S.T.

**1** Write the number 13.12 in the place value chart below.

| Hundreds | Tens | Ones | Tenths | Hundredths | Thousandths |
|---|---|---|---|---|---|
| | | | | | |

| | |
|---|---|
| Write a number that is ten times greater than 13.12. | |
| Write a number that is ten times less, or one-tenth of 13.12. | |

**2** Write the number 8.4 in the place value chart below.

| Hundreds | Tens | Ones | Tenths | Hundredths | Thousandths |
|---|---|---|---|---|---|
| | | | | | |

| | |
|---|---|
| Write a number that is ten times greater than 8.4. | |
| Write a number that is ten times less, or one-tenth of 8.4. | |

# TAKING ON THE B.E.S.T.

**1** Write the number 478 in the place value chart below.

| Hundreds | Tens | Ones | . | Tenths | Hundredths | Thousandths |
|---|---|---|---|---|---|---|
|  |  |  |  |  |  |  |

| | |
|---|---|
| Write a number that is 100 times greater than 478. |  |
| Write a number that is 10 times less than 478. |  |
| Write a number that is $\frac{1}{1000}$ of 478. |  |

**2** Write the number 9.1 in the place value chart below.

| Hundreds | Tens | Ones | Tenths | Hundredths | Thousandths |
|---|---|---|---|---|---|
|  |  |  |  |  |  |

| | |
|---|---|
| Write a number that is 1000 times greater than 9.1. |  |
| Write a number that is 10 times less than 9.1. |  |
| Write a number that is $\frac{1}{100}$ of 9.1. |  |

23

# TAKING ON THE B.E.S.T.

**1** Write the number 50 in the place value chart below.

| Hundreds | Tens | Ones | Tenths | Hundredths | Thousandths |
|----------|------|------|--------|------------|-------------|
|          |      |      |        |            |             |

| | |
|---|---|
| Write a number that is 100 times greater than 50. | |
| Write a number that is 10 times less than 50. | |
| Write a number that is $\frac{1}{1000}$ of 50. | |

**2** Write the number 10.4 in the place value chart below.

| Hundreds | Tens | Ones | Tenths | Hundredths | Thousandths |
|----------|------|------|--------|------------|-------------|
|          |      |      |        |            |             |

| | |
|---|---|
| Write a number that is 1000 times greater than 10.4. | |
| Write a number that is 10 times less than 10.4. | |
| Write a number that is $\frac{1}{100}$ of 10.4. | |

24

# TAKING ON THE B.E.S.T.

 Video Lesson

## True or False?

**1** Write the number 53 in the place value chart below. Then determine if each statement is true or false.

| Hundreds | Tens | Ones | Tenths | Hundredths | Thousandths |
|----------|------|------|--------|------------|-------------|
|          |      |      |        |            |             |

|                                          | TRUE OR FALSE? |
|------------------------------------------|----------------|
| 0.53 is ten times less than 53.          |                |
| 5,300 is 100 times greater than 53.      |                |
| 0.053 is $\frac{1}{1000}$ of 53.         |                |

**2** Write the number 640 in the place value chart below. Then determine if each statement is true or false.

| Hundreds | Tens | Ones | Tenths | Hundredths | Thousandths |
|----------|------|------|--------|------------|-------------|
|          |      |      |        |            |             |

|                                            | TRUE OR FALSE? |
|--------------------------------------------|----------------|
| 0.64 is one thousand times less than 640.  |                |
| 6,400 is ten times greater than 640.       |                |
| 6.4 is $\frac{1}{100}$ of 64.              |                |

# TAKING ON THE B.E.S.T.

| MA.5.NSO.1.1 | Extra Practice #3 | True or False? |

**1** Write the number 68 in the place value chart below. Then determine if each statement is true or false.

| Hundreds | Tens | Ones | Tenths | Hundredths | Thousandths |
|---|---|---|---|---|---|
| | | | | | |

| | TRUE OR FALSE? |
|---|---|
| 0.68 is ten times greater than 68. | |
| 6,800 is 100 times greater than 68. | |
| 0.068 is $\frac{1}{100}$ of 68. | |

**2** Write the number 7.1 in the place value chart below. Then determine if each statement is true or false.

| Hundreds | Tens | Ones | Tenths | Hundredths | Thousandths |
|---|---|---|---|---|---|
| | | | | | |

| | TRUE OR FALSE? |
|---|---|
| 0.71 is ten times less than 7.1. | |
| 7,100 is ten times greater than 7.1. | |
| 71 is $\frac{1}{10}$ of 7.1. | |

26

# TAKING ON THE B.E.S.T.

Yulia is purchasing supplies to make bracelets for her business. It costs $0.12 to make each bracelet. She sells each bracelet for $2.50.

## PART ONE

Help Yulia determine her supply costs by filling in the chart below:

| | TOTAL COST |
|---|---|
| How much will it cost to purchase supplies for 10 bracelets? | |
| How much will it cost to purchase supplies for 100 bracelets? | |
| How much will it cost to purchase supplies for 1,000 bracelets? | |

## PART TWO

Help Yulia determine how much she will earn in sales when she sells her bracelets by filling in the chart below:

| | TOTAL COST |
|---|---|
| How much will Yulia earn in sales for selling 10 bracelets? | |
| How much will Yulia earn in sales for selling 100 bracelets? | |
| How much will Yulia earn in sales for selling 1,000 bracelets? | |

27

# TAKING ON THE B.E.S.T.

## Math Misconception Mystery
### (PAGE 1)

**BEFORE THE VIDEO:** Solve the problem on your own.

What number is $\frac{1}{100}$ the value of 45?

**DURING THE VIDEO:** Pause after each "character" solves the problem and jot down quick notes to help you remember what they did correctly or incorrectly. .

Character #1 _____

Character #2 _____

Character #3 _____

Character #4 _____

# TAKING ON THE B.E.S.T.

| MA.5.NSO.1.1 | Math Misconception Mystery (PAGE 2) |
|---|---|

**AFTER THE VIDEO:** Discuss and analyze their answers.

The most reasonable answer belongs to Character # _____ because

_____

_____

_____

_____

(Justify how this character's work makes sense.)

## Let's help the others:

|  | Character #___: | Character #___: | Character #___: |
|---|---|---|---|
| What did this character do that was correct? |  |  |  |
| Identify their error |  |  |  |
| What do they need to know to understand for next time? |  |  |  |

29

# TAKING ON THE B.E.S.T.

Fill out the table to represent the number using the three different forms.

**1**

| STANDARD FORM | 983.256 | |
|---|---|---|
| WORD FORM | | |
| EXPANDED FORM | Strategy #1 | |
| | Strategy #2 | |

**2**

| STANDARD FORM | | |
|---|---|---|
| WORD FORM | | |
| EXPANDED FORM | Strategy #1<br>500 + 40 + 0.9+ 0.007 | |
| | Strategy #2 | |

# TAKING ON THE B.E.S.T.

**Extra Practice #1** **Read and Write Numbers with Decimals**

Fill out the table to represent the number using the three different forms.

## 1

| STANDARD FORM | |
|---|---|
| WORD FORM | **twenty-three and forty-six hundredths** |
| EXPANDED FORM | Strategy #1 |
| | Strategy #2 |

## 2

| STANDARD FORM | |
|---|---|
| WORD FORM | |
| EXPANDED FORM | Strategy #1 |
| | Strategy #2 $(6 \times 1{,}000) + (5 \times 10) + (4 \times \frac{1}{100})$ |

31

# TAKING ON THE B.E.S.T.

**Extra Practice #2**

## Read and Write Numbers with Decimals

Fill out the table to represent the number using the three different forms.

**1**

| STANDARD FORM | | |
|---|---|---|
| WORD FORM | | |
| EXPANDED FORM | Strategy #1 | **5,000 + 70 + 8 + 0.3 + 0.02 + 0.009** |
| | Strategy #2 | |

**2**

| STANDARD FORM | | 582,100.71 |
|---|---|---|
| WORD FORM | | |
| EXPANDED FORM | Strategy #1 | |
| | Strategy #2 | |

**MA.5.NSO.1.2** | **Extra Practice #3** | **Read and Write Numbers with Decimals**

Fill out the table to represent the number using the three different forms.

### 1

| STANDARD FORM | |
|---|---|
| WORD FORM | |
| EXPANDED FORM | Strategy #1 |
| | Strategy #2<br><br>$(8 \times 1{,}000) + (8 \times 100) + (5 \times 1) +$<br>$(5 \times \frac{1}{10}) + (2 \times \frac{1}{100}) + (3 \times \frac{1}{1000})$ |

### 2

| STANDARD FORM | |
|---|---|
| WORD FORM | **Two thousand, one hundred forty four and 12 thousandths** |
| EXPANDED FORM | Strategy #1 |
| | Strategy #2 |

# TAKING ON THE B.E.S.T.

| MA.5.NSO.1.2 | Math Missions | Read and Write Numbers with Decimals |

## PART ONE

Taylor has written a mysterious number on a piece of paper. Guess her number using the clues below:

CLUES:
- The digit in the ones place is one less than the digit in the thousandths place.
- The digit in the tens place is an even number between 1 and 5, but not 4.
- The digit in the hundredths place is equal to 400 divided by 100.
- The digit in the thousandths place is 8.

What is Taylor's number?

## PART TWO

Write Taylor's number in word form.

## PART THREE

Write Taylor's number in expanded form.

# TAKING ON THE B.E.S.T.

## Math Misconception Mystery (PAGE I)

**BEFORE THE VIDEO:** Solve the problem on your own.

> Write "eight hundred thirty-two and sixty six hundredths" in expanded form.

**DURING THE VIDEO:** Pause after each "character" solves the problem and jot down quick notes to help you remember what they did correctly or incorrectly. .

Character #1 _____

Character #2 _____

Character #3 _____

Character #4 _____

# TAKING ON THE B.E.S.T.

Math Misconception Mystery
(PAGE 2)

**AFTER THE VIDEO:** Discuss and analyze their answers.

The most reasonable answer belongs to Character # _____ because

_____

_____

_____

_____

(Justify how this character's work makes sense.)

## Let's help the others:

| | Character #___: | Character #___: | Character #___: |
|---|---|---|---|
| What did this character do that was correct? | | | |
| Identify their error | | | |
| What do they need to know to understand for next time? | | | |

36

# TAKING ON THE B.E.S.T.

**MA.5.NSO.1.3** | Video Lesson | **Decompose Numbers with Decimals**

Decompose each number two different ways and model each with place value blocks.

**1**

## 3.87

|  | EXPRESSION | DRAWING |
|---|---|---|
| **#1** |  |  |
| **#2** |  |  |

**2**

## 1.34

|  | EXPRESSION | DRAWING |
|---|---|---|
| **#1** |  |  |
| **#2** |  |  |

# TAKING ON THE B.E.S.T.

**Extra Practice #1** **Decompose Numbers with Decimals**

Decompose each number two different ways and model each with place value blocks.

## 1      2.01

| | EXPRESSION | DRAWING |
|---|---|---|
| #1 | | |
| #2 | | |

## 2      1.57

| | EXPRESSION | DRAWING |
|---|---|---|
| #1 | | |
| #2 | | |

# TAKING ON THE B.E.S.T.

Decompose each number two different ways and model each with place value blocks.

## 1  3.32

|     | EXPRESSION | DRAWING |
| --- | --- | --- |
| #1  |            |         |
| #2  |            |         |

## 2  4.9

|     | EXPRESSION | DRAWING |
| --- | --- | --- |
| #1  |            |         |
| #2  |            |         |

# TAKING ON THE B.E.S.T.

  Video Lesson | **Compose Numbers with Decimals**

Compose the values to determine the standard form of the number.

**1** 2 tens + 14 hundredths + 9 thousandths

**2** 410 tenths + 91 thousandths

**3** 62 tens + 45 hundredths + 7 thousandths

**4** 8 hundreds + 18 ones + 22 hundredths

# TAKING ON THE B.E.S.T.

Compose the values to determine the standard form of the number.

**1** 4 tens + 25 hundredths + 1 thousandths

**2** 522 ones + 31 hundredths

**3** 8 tens + 45 tenths + 77 thousandths

**4** 2 thousands + 18 tens + 18 tenths + 2 thousandths

# TAKING ON THE B.E.S.T.

| **Extra Practice #4** | **Compose Numbers with Decimals**

Compose the values to determine the standard form of the number.

**1** 65 tens + 340 hundredths

**2** 522 ones + 31 thousandths

**3** 5 hundreds + 451 tenths + 7 hundredths

**4** 12 thousands + 4 hundreds + 78 tenths + 89 thousandths

# TAKING ON THE B.E.S.T.

## PART ONE

Use the cards below to create a 4-digit number in the place value chart, only using each digit one time. Then, model your number by drawing place value blocks.

**CARDS**

6  3  2

4  9

| TENS | ONES | TENTHS | HUNDREDTHS |
|------|------|--------|------------|
|      |      |        |            |

Model with a drawing →

## PART TWO

Decompose your number two different ways.

## PART THREE

Martha decomposed her number as "34 ones + 96 hundredths." How do you write her number in standard form?

# TAKING ON THE B.E.S.T.

## Math Misconception Mystery
### (PAGE 1)

**BEFORE THE VIDEO:** Solve the problem on your own.

Select all the ways to name 12.129:
- Ⓐ 1 ten + 2 ones + 1 tenth + 2 hundredths + 9 thousandths
- Ⓑ 1 ten + 2 ones + 1 tenth + 2 hundredths + 9 ones
- Ⓒ 12 ones + 129 thousandths
- Ⓓ 121 hundredths + 2 tenths + 9 thousandths
- Ⓔ 121 tenths + 29 hundredths

**DURING THE VIDEO:** Pause after each "character" solves the problem and jot down quick notes to help you remember what they did correctly or incorrectly. .

| Character #1 _____ | Character #2 _____ |
|---|---|
| | |
| **Character #3** _____ | **Character #4** _____ |
| | |

# TAKING ON THE B.E.S.T.

**Math Misconception Mystery (PAGE 2)**

**AFTER THE VIDEO:** Discuss and analyze their answers.

The most reasonable answer belongs to Character # _____ because

_____

_____

_____

_____

(Justify how this character's work makes sense.)

## Let's help the others:

|  | Character #___: | Character #___: | Character #___: |
|---|---|---|---|
| What did this character do that was correct? |  |  |  |
| Identify their error |  |  |  |
| What do they need to know to understand for next time? |  |  |  |

**1** Plot each decimal number using the number line below. Then, order them from LEAST to GREATEST. Finally, complete the comparison statements with the correct symbol.

### 2.561; 2.57; 2.615

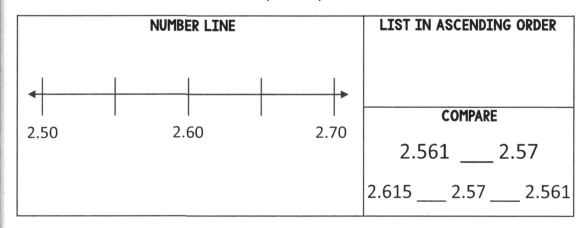

| NUMBER LINE | LIST IN ASCENDING ORDER |
|---|---|
| 2.50    2.60    2.70 | |
| | **COMPARE** |
| | 2.561 ___ 2.57 |
| | 2.615 ___ 2.57 ___ 2.561 |

**2** Plot each decimal number using the number line below. Then, order them from LEAST to GREATEST. Finally, complete the comparison statements with the correct symbol.

### 7.766; 7.776; 7.76

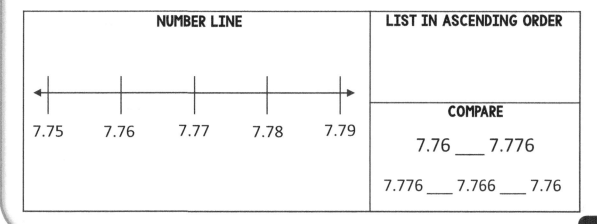

| NUMBER LINE | LIST IN ASCENDING ORDER |
|---|---|
| 7.75  7.76  7.77  7.78  7.79 | |
| | **COMPARE** |
| | 7.76 ___ 7.776 |
| | 7.776 ___ 7.766 ___ 7.76 |

46

# TAKING ON THE B.E.S.T.

**MA.5.NSO.1.4** | **Extra Practice #1** | **Plot, Order, and Compare Decimals (Number Line)**

**1** Plot each decimal number using the number line below. Then, order them from LEAST to GREATEST. Finally, complete the comparison statements with the correct symbol.

### 3.124; 3.241; 3.14

| NUMBER LINE | LIST IN ASCENDING ORDER |
|---|---|
| 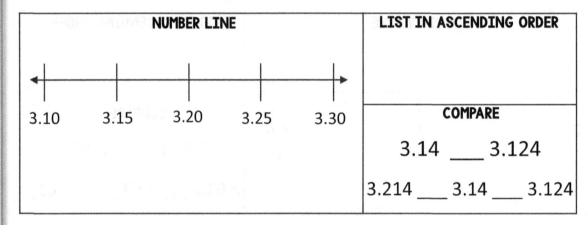 3.10  3.15  3.20  3.25  3.30 | |
| | **COMPARE** |
| | 3.14 ____ 3.124 |
| | 3.214 ____ 3.14 ____ 3.124 |

**2** Plot each decimal number using the number line below. Then, order them from LEAST to GREATEST. Finally, complete the comparison statements with the correct symbol.

### 5.023; 5.32; 5.203

| NUMBER LINE | LIST IN ASCENDING ORDER |
|---|---|
| 5.00  5.10  5.20  5.30  5.40 | |
| | **COMPARE** |
| | 5.023 ____ 5.32 |
| | 5.023 ____ 5.203 ____ 5.32 |

# TAKING ON THE B.E.S.T.

**1** Plot each decimal number using the number line below. Then, order them from LEAST to GREATEST. Finally, complete the comparison statements with the correct symbol.

### 9.447; 9.47; 9.474

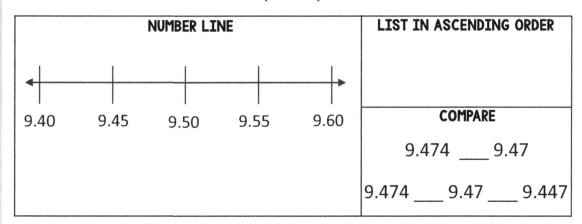

| NUMBER LINE | LIST IN ASCENDING ORDER |
|---|---|
| 9.40   9.45   9.50   9.55   9.60 | |
| | **COMPARE** |
| | 9.474 ___ 9.47 |
| | 9.474 ___ 9.47 ___ 9.447 |

**2** Plot each decimal number using the number line below. Then, order them from LEAST to GREATEST. Finally, complete the comparison statements with the correct symbol.

### 1.10; 1.01; 1.101

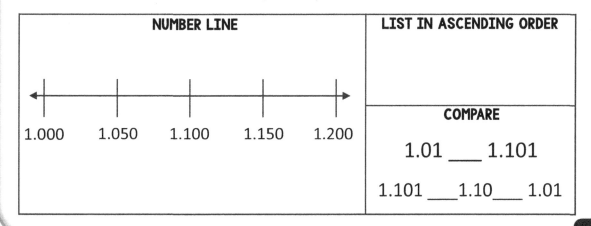

| NUMBER LINE | LIST IN ASCENDING ORDER |
|---|---|
| 1.000  1.050  1.100  1.150  1.200 | |
| | **COMPARE** |
| | 1.01 ___ 1.101 |
| | 1.101 ___ 1.10 ___ 1.01 |

48

# TAKING ON THE B.E.S.T.

**MA.5.NSO.1.4** | **Extra Practice #3** | **Plot, Order, and Compare Decimals (Number Line)**

**1** Plot each decimal number using the number line below. Then, order them from LEAST to GREATEST. Finally, complete the comparison statements with the correct symbol.

### 0.815; 0.851; 0.581

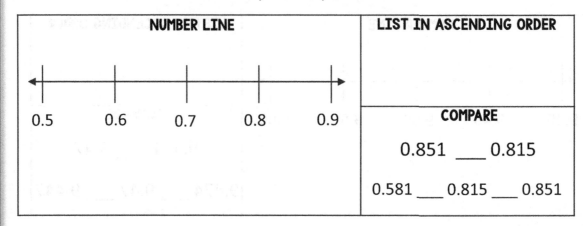

| NUMBER LINE | LIST IN ASCENDING ORDER |
|---|---|
| 0.5  0.6  0.7  0.8  0.9 | |
| | **COMPARE** |
| | 0.851 ___ 0.815 |
| | 0.581 ___ 0.815 ___ 0.851 |

**2** Plot each decimal number using the number line below. Then, order them from LEAST to GREATEST. Finally, complete the comparison statements with the correct symbol.

### 0.234; 0.34; 0.342

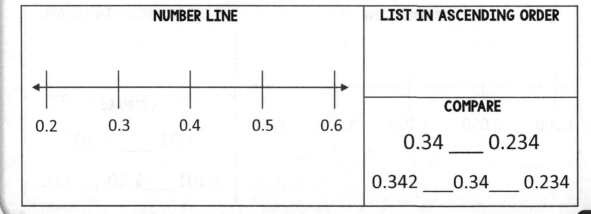

| NUMBER LINE | LIST IN ASCENDING ORDER |
|---|---|
| 0.2  0.3  0.4  0.5  0.6 | |
| | **COMPARE** |
| | 0.34 ___ 0.234 |
| | 0.342 ___ 0.34 ___ 0.234 |

# TAKING ON THE B.E.S.T.

| MA.5.NSO.1.4 | Math Missions | Plot, Order, and Compare Decimals |

Four students in Mrs. Thompson's class share how many hours they have volunteered this month. Nikkem has completed 4.55 hours, and Raul has completed 4.6 hours. Klaudia has completed 4.155 hours, and Todrick has completed 4.05 hours.

## PART ONE

Plot and label the students' times on the number line below.

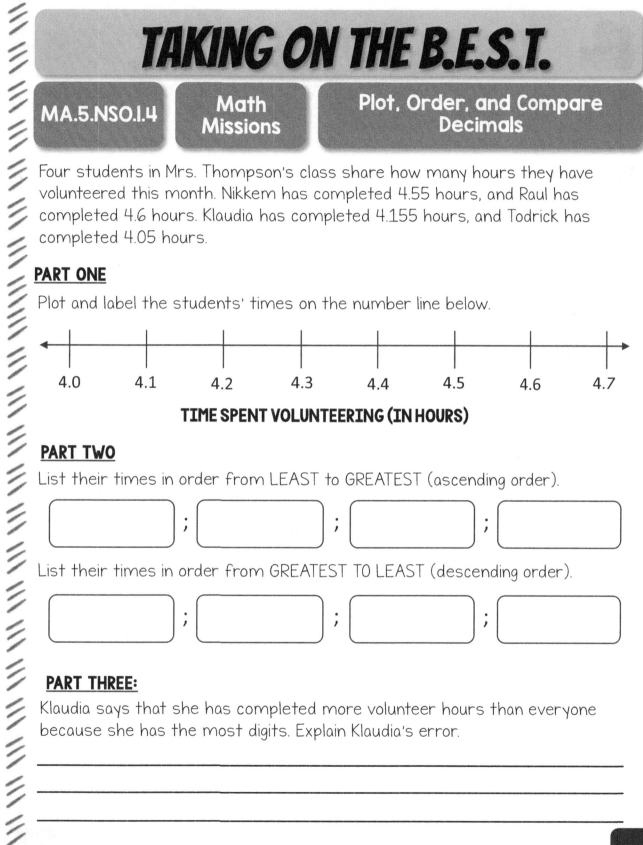

4.0    4.1    4.2    4.3    4.4    4.5    4.6    4.7

### TIME SPENT VOLUNTEERING (IN HOURS)

## PART TWO

List their times in order from LEAST to GREATEST (ascending order).

[   ] ; [   ] ; [   ] ; [   ]

List their times in order from GREATEST TO LEAST (descending order).

[   ] ; [   ] ; [   ] ; [   ]

## PART THREE:

Klaudia says that she has completed more volunteer hours than everyone because she has the most digits. Explain Klaudia's error.

_____

_____

_____

_____

# TAKING ON THE B.E.S.T.

## Math Misconception Mystery (PAGE I)

**BEFORE THE VIDEO:** Solve the problem on your own.

Select all the values that would make the following comparison a true statement.

$$1.34 < \underline{\hspace{2cm}}$$

Ⓐ 1.340
Ⓑ 1.314
Ⓒ 1.4
Ⓓ 1.334
Ⓔ 13.0

**DURING THE VIDEO:** Pause after each "character" solves the problem and jot down quick notes to help you remember what they did correctly or incorrectly. .

| Character #1 _____ | Character #2 _____ |
|---|---|
| | |
| Character #3 _____ | Character #4 _____ |
| | |

# TAKING ON THE B.E.S.T.

## Math Misconception Mystery
### (PAGE 2)

**AFTER THE VIDEO:** Discuss and analyze their answers.

The most reasonable answer belongs to Character # _____ because

_____

_____

_____

_____

(Justify how this character's work makes sense.)

## Let's help the others:

| | Character #___: | Character #___: | Character #___: |
|---|---|---|---|
| What did this character do that was correct? | | | |
| Identify their error | | | |
| What do they need to know to understand for next time? | | | |

# TAKING ON THE B.E.S.T.

  **Video Lesson** **Round to the Nearest Tenth and Hundredth**

**1** Round 3.317 to the nearest tenth and hundredth. Use a number line and place value strategies to show your thinking.

|  | Nearest Tenth | Nearest Hundredth |
|---|---|---|
| Number Line |  |  |
| Place Value |  |  |

**2** Round 8.726 to the nearest tenth and hundredth. Use a number line and place value strategies to show your thinking.

|  | Nearest Tenth | Nearest Hundredth |
|---|---|---|
| Number Line |  |  |
| Place Value |  |  |

**3** Round 9.534 to the nearest tenth and hundredth. Use a number line and place value strategies to show your thinking.

|  | Nearest Tenth | Nearest Hundredth |
|---|---|---|
| Number Line |  |  |
| Place Value |  |  |

# TAKING ON THE B.E.S.T.

| MA.5.NSO.1.5 | Extra Practice #1 | Round to the Nearest Tenth and Hundredth |
|---|---|---|

**1** Round 4.681 to the nearest tenth and hundredth. Use a number line and place value strategies to show your thinking.

|  | Nearest Tenth | Nearest Hundredth |
|---|---|---|
| Number Line |  |  |
| Place Value |  |  |

**2** Round 7.617 to the nearest tenth and hundredth. Use a number line and place value strategies to show your thinking.

|  | Nearest Tenth | Nearest Hundredth |
|---|---|---|
| Number Line |  |  |
| Place Value |  |  |

**3** Round 10.443 to the nearest tenth and hundredth. Use a number line and place value strategies to show your thinking.

|  | Nearest Tenth | Nearest Hundredth |
|---|---|---|
| Number Line |  |  |
| Place Value |  |  |

# TAKING ON THE B.E.S.T.

**1** Round 7.654 to the nearest whole and tenth. Use a number line and place value strategies to show your thinking.

| | Nearest Whole | Nearest Tenth |
|---|---|---|
| Number Line | | |
| Place Value | | |

**2** Round 5.257 to the nearest whole and hundredth. Use a number line and place value strategies to show your thinking.

| | Nearest Whole | Nearest Hundredth |
|---|---|---|
| Number Line | | |
| Place Value | | |

**3** Round 9.989 to the nearest whole and tenth. Use a number line and and place value strategies to show your thinking.

| | Nearest Whole | Nearest Tenth |
|---|---|---|
| Number Line | | |
| Place Value | | |

# TAKING ON THE B.E.S.T.

**1** Round 6.765 to the nearest whole and tenth. Use a number line and and place value strategies to show your thinking.

|  | Nearest Whole | Nearest Tenth |
|---|---|---|
| Number Line |  |  |
| Place Value |  |  |

**2** Round 4.166 to the nearest whole and hundredth. Use a number line and place value strategies to show your thinking.

|  | Nearest Whole | Nearest Hundredth |
|---|---|---|
| Number Line |  |  |
| Place Value |  |  |

**3** Round 3.537 to the nearest whole and tenth. Use a number line and place value strategies to show your thinking.

|  | Nearest Whole | Nearest Tenth |
|---|---|---|
| Number Line |  |  |
| Place Value |  |  |

# TAKING ON THE B.E.S.T.

 Video Lesson

## Estimating Sums and Differences

**1** Use rounding to estimate the sum of 6.234 and 3.171.

**2** Use rounding to estimate the difference of 9.982 from 47.13.

**3** Use rounding to estimate the sum of 4.828 and 2.11. Then, estimate the difference of 2.11 from 4.828.

# TAKING ON THE B.E.S.T.

**1** Use rounding to estimate the sum of 3.316 and 4.892.

**2** Use rounding to estimate the difference of 13.777 from 59.83.

**3** Use rounding to estimate the sum of 26.309 and 8.22. Then, estimate the difference of 8.22 from 26.309.

# TAKING ON THE B.E.S.T.

| MA.5.NSO.1.5 | Math Mission | Rounding to the Nearest Whole, Tenth, and Hundredth |

## PART ONE

Roger is thinking of a 5–digit number with decimals to the thousandths place. He provides clues to his number.

CLUES:

*   Roger's number rounded to the nearest whole is 39.
*   Roger's number rounded to the nearest hundredth is 39.16.
*   The digit in the thousandths place is odd and has a value between 0.004 and 0.006.

## PART TWO

What is Roger's number rounded to the nearest tenth? Use the number line to explain your thinking.

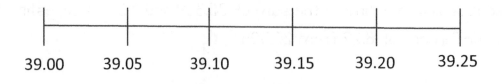

39.00    39.05    39.10    39.15    39.20    39.25

_____

_____

_____

_____

# TAKING ON THE B.E.S.T.

## Math Misconception Mystery (PAGE 1)

**BEFORE THE VIDEO:** Solve the problem on your own.

> Brianna has $72.83 in her savings account. Round this amount to the nearest whole and tenth.

**DURING THE VIDEO:** Pause after each "character" solves the problem and jot down quick notes to help you remember what they did correctly or incorrectly. .

| Character #1 _____ | Character #2 _____ |
|---|---|
| | |
| **Character #3** _____ | **Character #4** _____ |
| | |

# TAKING ON THE B.E.S.T.

**Math Misconception Mystery (PAGE 2)**

**AFTER THE VIDEO:** Discuss and analyze their answers.

The most reasonable answer belongs to Character # _____ because

_____

_____

_____

_____

(Justify how this character's work makes sense.)

## Let's help the others:

|  | Character #___: | Character #___: | Character #___: |
|---|---|---|---|
| What did this character do that was correct? |  |  |  |
| Identify their error |  |  |  |
| What do they need to know to understand for next time? |  |  |  |

# TAKING ON THE B.E.S.T.

 Video Lesson

## Multiply Whole Numbers By 1 Digit

**1** 4,836 x 7 | **ESTIMATE:**

STANDARD ALGORITHM

**2** 51,209 x 8 | **ESTIMATE:**

STANDARD ALGORITHM

# TAKING ON THE B.E.S.T.

**1**   2,914 x 6   **ESTIMATE:**

**STANDARD ALGORITHM**

**2**   33,579 x 4   **ESTIMATE:**

**STANDARD ALGORITHM**

MA.5.NSO.2.I  Video Lesson | **Multiply Whole Numbers By 2 Digits**

**1** 7,329 x 18 | ESTIMATE:

**STANDARD ALGORITHM**

**2** 46,083 x 32 | ESTIMATE:

**STANDARD ALGORITHM**

# TAKING ON THE B.E.S.T.

**1**  5,507 x 36     ESTIMATE:

STANDARD ALGORITHM

**2**  24,205 x 54     ESTIMATE:

STANDARD ALGORITHM

# TAKING ON THE B.E.S.T.

  **Video Lesson** **Multiply Whole Numbers By 3 Digits**

**1** 6,914 x 281     ESTIMATE:

**STANDARD ALGORITHM**

**2** 465 x 329     ESTIMATE:

**STANDARD ALGORITHM**

# TAKING ON THE B.E.S.T.

**MA.5.NSO.2.1** | **Extra Practice #3** | **Multiply Whole Numbers By 3 Digits**

**1**    4,792 x 370    **ESTIMATE:**

**STANDARD ALGORITHM**

**2**    198 x 145    **ESTIMATE:**

**STANDARD ALGORITHM**

# TAKING ON THE B.E.S.T.

**MA.5.NSO.2.1** | **Math Missions** | **Multiply Whole Numbers**

## PART ONE

Use each card one time to multiply a 3-digit whole number by 2- digit whole number to create a  product less than 23,000.

### CARDS

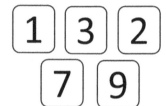

## PART TWO

Claire uses the cards to create the expression 91 x 723 and believes that this arrangement creates the greatest possible product. Do you agree with Claire? Explain your thinking.

_____

_____

_____

_____

# TAKING ON THE B.E.S.T.

## Math Misconception Mystery
## (PAGE 1)

**BEFORE THE VIDEO:** Solve the problem on your own.

> What is the product of 2,479 and 68?

**DURING THE VIDEO:** Pause after each "character" solves the problem and jot down quick notes to help you remember what they did correctly or incorrectly. .

Character #1 _____

Character #2 _____

Character #3 _____

Character #4 _____

**MA.5.NSO.2.1** — **Math Misconception Mystery (PAGE 2)**

**AFTER THE VIDEO:** Discuss and analyze their answers.

The most reasonable answer belongs to Character # _____ because

_____

_____

_____

_____

(Justify how this character's work makes sense.)

## Let's help the others:

| | Character #___: | Character #___: | Character #___: |
|---|---|---|---|
| What did this character do that was correct? | | | |
| Identify their error | | | |
| What do they need to know to understand for next time? | | | |

MA.5.NSO.2.2  Video Lesson | Divide Up to 5-Digits By 2-Digits (Area Model)

**1** 1,367 ÷ 23 | ESTIMATE:

AREA MODEL | CHECK USING MULTIPLICATION

**2** 21,284 ÷ 67 | ESTIMATE:

AREA MODEL | CHECK USING MULTIPLICATION

| MA.5.NSO.2.2 | Extra Practice #1 | Divide Up to 5-Digits By 2-Digits (Area Model) |

**1**    $4,037 \div 38$    ESTIMATE:

AREA MODEL

CHECK USING MULTIPLICATION

**2**    $32,855 \div 36$    ESTIMATE:

AREA MODEL

CHECK USING MULTIPLICATION

## 1   2,537 ÷ 44     ESTIMATE:

**AREA MODEL**

**CHECK USING MULTIPLICATION**

## 2   36,855 ÷ 72     ESTIMATE:

**AREA MODEL**

**CHECK USING MULTIPLICATION**

# TAKING ON THE B.E.S.T.

**MA.5.NSO.2.2**     **Video Lesson**    **Divide Up to 5-Digits By 2-Digits (Partial Quotients)**

## 1.  81,702 ÷ 84

**ESTIMATE:**

| PARTIAL QUOTIENTS | CHECK USING MULTIPLICATION |
|---|---|
|  |  |

## 2.  53,113 ÷ 85

**ESTIMATE:**

| PARTIAL QUOTIENTS | CHECK USING MULTIPLICATION |
|---|---|
|  |  |

74

| MA.5.NSO.2.2 | Extra Practice #3 | Divide Up to 5-Digits By 2-Digits (Partial Quotients) |

**1**  8,702 ÷ 73

ESTIMATE:

| PARTIAL QUOTIENTS | CHECK USING MULTIPLICATION |

**2**  66,234 ÷ 22

ESTIMATE:

| PARTIAL QUOTIENTS | CHECK USING MULTIPLICATION |

# TAKING ON THE B.E.S.T.

| Extra Practice #4 | Divide Up to 5-Digits By 2-Digits (Partial Quotients)

## 1. $30,087 \div 48$

ESTIMATE:

| PARTIAL QUOTIENTS | CHECK USING MULTIPLICATION |
|---|---|
| | |

## 2. $46,009 \div 67$

ESTIMATE:

| PARTIAL QUOTIENTS | CHECK USING MULTIPLICATION |
|---|---|
| | |

MA.5.NSO.2.2 |  Video Lesson | **Divide Up to 5-Digits By 2-Digits (Long Division Algorithm)**

**1**   73,702 ÷ 82    ESTIMATE:

| LONG DIVISION ALGORITHM | CHECK USING MULTIPLICATION |
|---|---|
| | |

**2**   2,177 ÷ 73    ESTIMATE:

| LONG DIVISION ALGORITHM | CHECK USING MULTIPLICATION |
|---|---|
| | |

**1** 65,831 ÷ 78

ESTIMATE:

| LONG DIVISION ALGORITHM | CHECK USING MULTIPLICATION |
| --- | --- |
| | |

**2** 25,037 ÷ 42

ESTIMATE:

| LONG DIVISION ALGORITHM | CHECK USING MULTIPLICATION |
| --- | --- |
| | |

# TAKING ON THE B.E.S.T.

**1** 59,054 ÷ 28

ESTIMATE:

| LONG DIVISION ALGORITHM | CHECK USING MULTIPLICATION |
|---|---|
| | |

**2** 3,099 ÷ 41

ESTIMATE:

| LONG DIVISION ALGORITHM | CHECK USING MULTIPLICATION |
|---|---|
| | |

# TAKING ON THE B.E.S.T.

**MA.5.NSO.2.2** | **Math Missions** | **Divide Up to 5-Digits By 2-Digits**

## PART ONE

Use each card one time to create a division problem that has a quotient of more than 70. Show how you can find the exact quotient.

### CARDS

$$\boxed{\phantom{0}}\boxed{\phantom{0}}\boxed{\phantom{0}}\boxed{\phantom{0}} \div \boxed{\phantom{0}}\boxed{\phantom{0}}$$

## PART TWO

Francesca says that 6,923 divided by 57 will provide a quotient of exactly 121. Explain how her theory is incorrect.

_____

_____

_____

_____

80

# TAKING ON THE B.E.S.T.

## Math Misconception Mystery (PAGE 1)

**BEFORE THE VIDEO:** Solve the problem on your own.

Find the quotient of 4,098 divided by 44.

**DURING THE VIDEO:** Pause after each "character" solves the problem and jot down quick notes to help you remember what they did correctly or incorrectly. .

Character #1 _____

Character #2 _____

Character #3 _____

Character #4 _____

81

# TAKING ON THE B.E.S.T.

## Math Misconception Mystery (PAGE 2)

**AFTER THE VIDEO:** Discuss and analyze their answers.

The most reasonable answer belongs to Character # _____ because
_____
_____
_____
_____

(Justify how this character's work makes sense.)

### Let's help the others:

|  | Character #___: | Character #___: | Character #___: |
|---|---|---|---|
| What did this character do that was correct? |  |  |  |
| Identify their error |  |  |  |
| What do they need to know to understand for next time? |  |  |  |

# TAKING ON THE B.E.S.T.

MA.5.NSO.2.3  Video Lesson

## Addition with Decimals: Standard Algorithm

Estimate the sum. Then use a standard algorithm (based on place value) to solve.

**1** 20.721 + 2.029 | ESTIMATE:

**2** 16.88 + 3.997 | ESTIMATE:

Estimate the sum. Then use a standard algorithm (based on place value) to solve.

**1** 18.394 + 5.21    ESTIMATE:

**2** 15.018 + 5.97    ESTIMATE:

# TAKING ON THE B.E.S.T.

**MA.5.NSO.2.3**  Video Lesson | **Subtraction with Decimals: Standard Algorithm**

Estimate the difference. Then use a standard algorithm (based on place value) to solve.

 **1** 20.72 – 2.024 | **ESTIMATE:**

**2** 16.88 – 3.99 | **ESTIMATE:**

# TAKING ON THE B.E.S.T.

**Extra Practice #2**

**Subtraction with Decimals: Standard Algorithm**

Estimate the difference. Then use a standard algorithm (based on place value) to solve.

**1** 18.379 – 5.813   **ESTIMATE:**

**2** 7.01 – 5.973   **ESTIMATE:**

# TAKING ON THE B.E.S.T.

**MA.5.NSO.2.3** | **Math Missions** | **Adding & Subtracting Numbers with Decimals**

## PART ONE

Misha runs two 100-meter races. She completes her first race in 10.619 seconds. She completes her second race 0.78 second slower. What was her time for her second race? Explain your answer.

_____

_____

_____

_____

## PART TWO

Estefan runs two 200-meter races. He completes his first race in 23.081 seconds. He completes his second race in 25.29 seconds. How much faster did he complete his first race? Explain your answer.

_____

_____

_____

_____

# TAKING ON THE B.E.S.T.

## Math Misconception Mystery
### (PAGE 1)

**BEFORE THE VIDEO:** Solve the problem on your own.

Estimate, then solve:   34.11 - 2.997

**DURING THE VIDEO:** Pause after each "character" solves the problem and jot down quick notes to help you remember what they did correctly or incorrectly. .

| Character #1 _____ | Character #2 _____ |
|---|---|
| | |
| **Character #3** _____ | **Character #4** _____ |
| | |

# TAKING ON THE B.E.S.T.

**Math Misconception Mystery (PAGE 2)**

**AFTER THE VIDEO:** Discuss and analyze their answers.

The most reasonable answer belongs to Character # _____ because

_____

_____

_____

_____

(Justify how this character's work makes sense.)

## Let's help the others:

| | Character #___: | Character #___: | Character #___: |
|---|---|---|---|
| What did this character do that was correct? | | | |
| Identify their error | | | |
| What do they need to know to understand for next time? | | | |

# TAKING ON THE B.E.S.T.

 **MA.5.NSO.2.4** | **Video Lesson** | **Exploring Multiplication with Decimals**

Use place value relationships to explore multiplication with decimals.

**1** Model each multiplication expression with a drawing to solve.

| 5 x 4 | 5 x 0.4 | 0.5 x 0.4 |
|---|---|---|
| | | 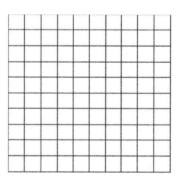 |

**2** Model each multiplication expression with a drawing to solve.

| 7 x 3 | 7 x 0.3 | 0.7 x 0.3 |
|---|---|---|
| | | 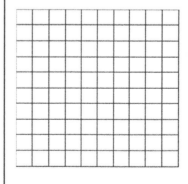 |

What do you notice about the placement of the decimal?

_____

_____

_____

**MA.5.NSO.2.4** | **Extra Practice #1** | **Exploring Multiplication with Decimals**

Use place value relationships to explore multiplication with decimals.

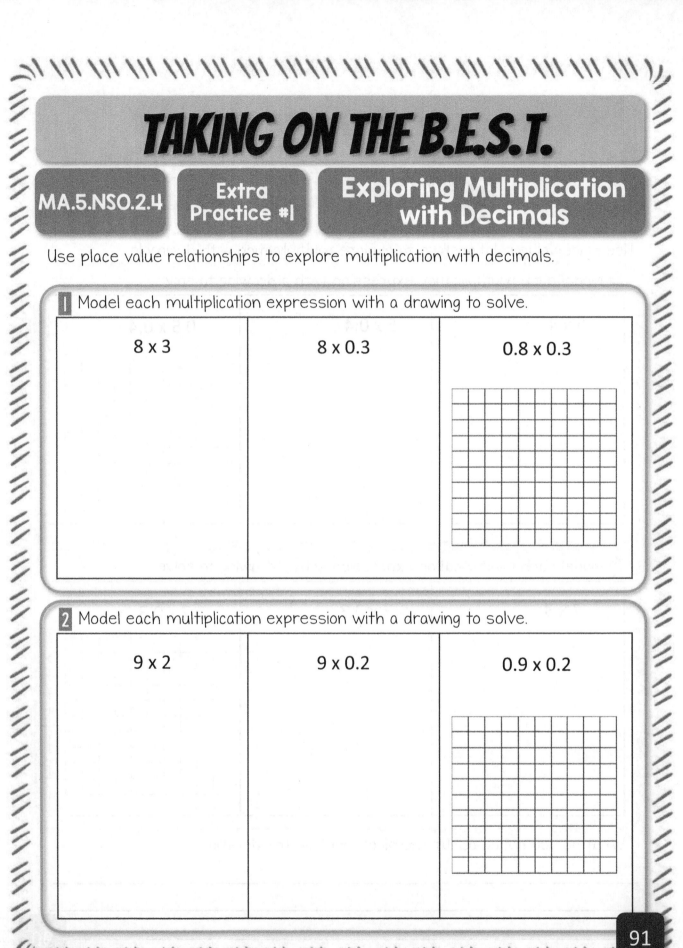

**1** Model each multiplication expression with a drawing to solve.

| 8 x 3 | 8 x 0.3 | 0.8 x 0.3 |
|---|---|---|

**2** Model each multiplication expression with a drawing to solve.

| 9 x 2 | 9 x 0.2 | 0.9 x 0.2 |
|---|---|---|

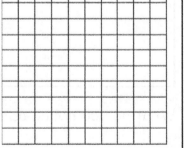

# TAKING ON THE B.E.S.T.

Use place value relationships to explore division with decimals.

1 Model each division expression with a drawing to solve.

| 24 ÷ 6 | 24 ÷ 0.6 | 2.4 ÷ 0.6 |
|---|---|---|
| | 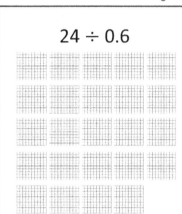 | 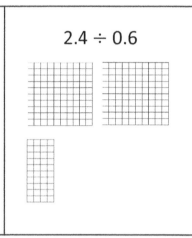 |

2 Model each division expression with a drawing to solve.

| 10 ÷ 5 | 10 ÷ 0.5 | 1.0 ÷ 0.5 |
|---|---|---|
| 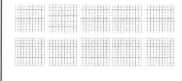 |  |  |

What do you notice about the placement of the decimal?

_____

_____

_____

# TAKING ON THE B.E.S.T.

**MA.5.NSO.2.4** | **Extra Practice #2** | **Exploring Division with Decimals**

Use place value relationships to explore division with decimals.

**1** Model each division expression with a drawing to solve.

| $8 \div 4$ | $8 \div 0.4$ | $0.8 \div 0.4$ |
|---|---|---|
| 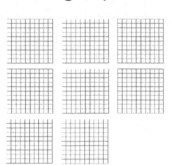 | 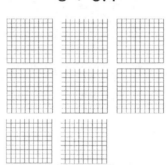 | 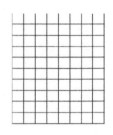 |

**2** Model each division expression with a drawing to solve.

| $12 \div 2$ | $12 \div 0.2$ | $1.2 \div 0.2$ |
|---|---|---|
| 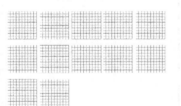 | 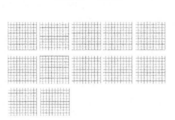 | 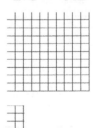 |

# TAKING ON THE B.E.S.T.

  **Video Lesson** | **Using Estimation to Multiply Numbers with Decimals**

First, estimate the value of each expression. Then, multiply to find the exact product.

**1** 4 × 0.8

ESTIMATE:

**2** 0.7 × 0.9

ESTIMATE:

94

# TAKING ON THE B.E.S.T.

**Extra Practice #3**

## Using Estimation to Multiply Numbers with Decimals

First, estimate the value of each expression. Then, multiply to find the exact product.

 6.1 x 2.5

**ESTIMATE:**

 7.2 x 1.2

**ESTIMATE:**

# TAKING ON THE B.E.S.T.

## Using Estimation to Divide Numbers with Decimals

First, estimate the value of each expression. Then, division to find the exact quotient.

**1** 12 ÷ 1.2

ESTIMATE:

**2** 18 ÷ 0.6

ESTIMATE:

# TAKING ON THE B.E.S.T.

**MA.5.NSO.2.4** | **Extra Practice #4** | **Using Estimation to Divide Numbers with Decimals**

First, estimate the value of each expression. Then, division to find the exact quotient.

 $25 \div 0.5$

ESTIMATE:

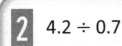 $4.2 \div 0.7$

ESTIMATE:

97

# TAKING ON THE B.E.S.T.

| MA.5.NSO.2.4 | Math Missions | Exploring Multiplication and Division with Decimals |
|---|---|---|

## PART ONE

Explain how you can use the expression 7 x 4 to help you solve 7 x 0.4.

_____

_____

_____

_____

## PART TWO

Model 7 x 0.4 with a drawing to find the product.

## PART THREE

Shaquane says that 2.8 divided by 0.4 is 70 because she used 28 divided by 4 to determine the quotient. Explain how Shaquane could use estimation to determine that 70 is not a reasonable answer.

_____

_____

_____

_____

# TAKING ON THE B.E.S.T.

## Math Misconception Mystery
### (PAGE 1)

**BEFORE THE VIDEO:** Solve the problem on your own.

Find the product of 0.8 x 2.

**DURING THE VIDEO:** Pause after each "character" solves the problem and jot down quick notes to help you remember what they did correctly or incorrectly. .

Character #1 _____

Character #2 _____

Character #3 _____

Character #4 _____

# TAKING ON THE B.E.S.T.

## Math Misconception Mystery
## (PAGE 2)

**AFTER THE VIDEO:** Discuss and analyze their answers.

The most reasonable answer belongs to Character # _____ because

_____

_____

_____

_____

(Justify how this character's work makes sense.)

### Let's help the others:

|  | Character #___: | Character #___: | Character #___: |
|---|---|---|---|
| What did this character do that was correct? |  |  |  |
| Identify their error |  |  |  |
| What do they need to know to understand for next time? |  |  |  |

100

# TAKING ON THE B.E.S.T.

Multiply each number by 0.1 and 0.01. Use a place value chart to demonstrate how to solve each problem.

**1**

| 5.4 x 0.1 = _____ | 5.4 x 0.01 = _____ |
|---|---|
| You can also write the equation as | You can also write the equation as |
| 5.4 x _____ = _____ | 5.4 x _____ = _____ |

**2**

| 10.6 x 0.1 = _____ | 10.6 x 0.01 = _____ |
|---|---|
| You can also write the equation as | You can also write the equation as |
| 10.6 x _____ = _____ | 10.6 x _____ = _____ |

# TAKING ON THE B.E.S.T.

| Extra Practice #1 | Multiply by 0.1 and 0.01 ($\frac{1}{10}$ and $\frac{1}{100}$)

Multiply each number by 0.1 and 0.01. Use a place value chart to demonstrate how to solve each problem.

**1**

| | |
|---|---|
| 6.3 x 0.1 = _____ | 6.3 x 0.01 = _____ |
| You can also write the equation as | You can also write the equation as |
| 6.3 x _____ = _____ | 6.3 x _____ = _____ |

**2**

| | |
|---|---|
| 25.1 x 0.1 = _____ | 25.1 x 0.01 = _____ |
| You can also write the equation as | You can also write the equation as |
| 25.1 x _____ = _____ | 25.1 x _____ = _____ |

# TAKING ON THE B.E.S.T.

Divide each number by 0.1 and 0.01. Use a place value chart to demonstrate how to solve each problem.

**1**

6.5 ÷ 0.1 = _____

6.5 ÷ 0.01 = _____

You can also write the equation as
6.5 ÷ _____ = _____

You can also write the equation as
6.5 ÷ _____ = _____

**2**

21.4 ÷ 0.1 = _____

21.4 ÷ 0.01 = _____

You can also write the equation as
21.4 ÷ _____ = _____

You can also write the equation as
21.4 ÷ _____ = _____

# TAKING ON THE B.E.S.T.

**Extra Practice #2** **Dividing by 0.1 and 0.01 ($\frac{1}{10}$ and $\frac{1}{100}$)**

Divide each number by 0.1 and 0.01. Use a place value chart to demonstrate how to solve each problem.

**1**

$18.9 \div 0.1 =$ _____

$18.9 \div 0.01 =$ _____

You can also write the equation as
$18.9 \div$ _____ $=$ _____

You can also write the equation as
$18.9 \div$ _____ $=$ _____

**2**

$0.6 \div 0.1 =$ _____

$0.6 \div 0.01 =$ _____

You can also write the equation as
$0.6 \div$ _____ $=$ _____

You can also write the equation as
$0.6 \div$ _____ $=$ _____

# TAKING ON THE B.E.S.T.

Fill in the blanks to complete each statement.

**1** The product of 3.7 x 0.1 is _____ times _____ than the product of 3.7 x 0.01.

**2** The quotient of 17.7 ÷ 0.01 is _____ times _____ than the quotient of 17.7 ÷ 0.1.

**3** The product of 13.6 x 0.01 is _____ times _____ than the product of 13.6 x 0.1.

**4** The quotient of 8.4 ÷ 0.01 is _____ times _____ than the quotient of 8.4 ÷ 0.1.

**5** The product of 5.5 x 0.1 is _____ times _____ than the product of 5.5 x 10.

# TAKING ON THE B.E.S.T.

Fill in the blanks to complete each statement.

**1** The product of 5.2 x 0.1 is _____ times _____ than the product of 5.2 x 0.01.

**2** The quotient of 18.3 ÷ 0.01 is _____ times _____ than the quotient of 18.3 ÷ 0.1.

**3** The product of 98.3 x 0.01 is _____ times _____ than the product of 98.3 x 0.1.

**4** The quotient of 10.1 ÷ 0.01 is _____ times _____ than the quotient of 10.1 ÷ 0.1.

**5** The product of 4.2 x 0.1 is _____ times _____ than the product of 4.2 x 10.

# TAKING ON THE B.E.S.T.

**MA.5.NSO.2.5** | **Math Missions** | **Multiplying and Dividing by 0.1 and 0.01**

Lamar has $2.60 in his wallet.

## PART ONE

How many dimes are in $2.60?

## PART TWO

How many pennies are in $2.60?

## PART THREE

Christina has $26.00. She says that she has 100 times more than Lamar. Do you agree with Christina's statement? Explain your thinking.

# TAKING ON THE B.E.S.T.

## MA.5.NSO.2.5 | Math Misconception Mystery (PAGE 1)

**BEFORE THE VIDEO:** Solve the problem on your own.

Fill in the blanks to make the statement true:

The product of 4.6 x 0.01 is _____ times _____ than the product of 4.6 x 0.1.

**DURING THE VIDEO:** Pause after each "character" solves the problem and jot down quick notes to help you remember what they did correctly or incorrectly. .

| Character #1 _____ | Character #2 _____ |
|---|---|
| Character #3 _____ | Character #4 _____ |

# TAKING ON THE B.E.S.T.

## Math Misconception Mystery (PAGE 2)

**AFTER THE VIDEO:** Discuss and analyze their answers.

The most reasonable answer belongs to Character # _____ because

_____

_____

_____

_____

(Justify how this character's work makes sense.)

### Let's help the others:

| | Character #___: | Character #___: | Character #___: |
|---|---|---|---|
| What did this character do that was correct? | | | |
| Identify their error | | | |
| What do they need to know to understand for next time? | | | |

# TAKING ON THE B.E.S.T.

Represent each division expression as a fraction. Model with a visual area model.

**1** $12 \div 4$

**2** $4 \div 12$

**3** $7 \div 8$

**4** $8 \div 7$

# TAKING ON THE B.E.S.T.

**MA.5.FR.I.I** | **Extra Practice #1** | **Represent Division of Two Whole Numbers as a Fraction**

Represent each division expression as a fraction. Model with a visual area model.

**1** $18 \div 6$

**2** $6 \div 18$

**3** $4 \div 5$

**4** $5 \div 4$

# TAKING ON THE B.E.S.T.

 **Video Lesson**

**Division as Fractions** (Less Than One) **Real World Problems**

Represent each division expression as a fraction. Model with a visual area model.

**1** Juan has six whole pizzas. He shares them among himself and his nine friends. How much pizza does each person receive?

**2** Ella has 10 feet of wood. She cuts the wood into 12 equal pieces. How long is each piece of wood?

**3** Shaniece has 5 gallons of lemonade. She pours the lemonade into 7 equal-sized containers. How much lemonade is in each container, in gallons?

# TAKING ON THE B.E.S.T.

Represent each division expression as a fraction. Model with a visual area model.

**1** There are 3 graham crackers in a box. Teddy puts an equal amount of graham crackers on 5 plates. How much of a whole graham cracker was on each plate?

**2** Derek realizes that he only has four cups on laundry detergent left. He has nine loads of laundry that he must complete. If he uses the same of amount of laundry detergent, how much will he use for each load, in cups?

**3** Lucy has 5 feet of string. She cuts the string into 12 equal-sized pieces. What is the length of each piece of string?

# TAKING ON THE B.E.S.T.

Represent each division expression as a fraction. Model with a visual area model.

**1** Juan has 10 whole pizzas. He shares them among himself and his five friends. How much pizza does each person receive?

**2** Ella has 12 feet of wood. She cuts the wood into 10 equal pieces. How long is each piece of wood?

**3** Shaniece has 7 gallons of lemonade. She pours the lemonade into 5 equal-sized containers. How much lemonade is in each container, in gallons?

# TAKING ON THE B.E.S.T.

Represent each division expression as a fraction. Model with a visual area model.

**1** There are 5 graham crackers in a box. Teddy puts an equal amount of graham crackers on 3 plates. How much of a whole graham cracker was on each plate?

**2** Derek realizes that he only has nine cups on laundry detergent left. He has four loads of laundry that he must complete. If he uses the same of amount of laundry detergent, how much will he use for each load, in cups?

**3** Lucy has 12 feet of string. She cuts the string into 5 equal-sized pieces. What is the length of each piece of string?

# TAKING ON THE B.E.S.T.

**MA.5.FR.I.I** | **Math Missions** | **Represent Division of Two Whole Numbers as a Fraction**

## PART ONE

Write 3 ÷ 8 as a fraction.

## PART TWO

Model 3 ÷ 8 with a drawing.

## PART THREE

Create your own real-world problem for 3 ÷ 8.

_____

_____

_____

_____

_____

# TAKING ON THE B.E.S.T.

## MA.5.FR.1.1 | Math Misconception Mystery (PAGE 1)

**BEFORE THE VIDEO:** Solve the problem on your own.

> Jericho has 10 double-fudge chocolate brownies that need to be distributed equally among 6 people. How many brownies will each person receive?

**DURING THE VIDEO:** Pause after each "character" solves the problem and jot down quick notes to help you remember what they did correctly or incorrectly.

| Character #1 _____ | Character #2 _____ |
|---|---|
| | |
| **Character #3** _____ | **Character #4** _____ |
| | |

117

# TAKING ON THE B.E.S.T.

## Math Misconception Mystery
### (PAGE 2)

**AFTER THE VIDEO:** Discuss and analyze their answers.

The most reasonable answer belongs to Character # _____ because

_____

_____

_____

_____

(Justify how this character's work makes sense.)

## Let's help the others:

| | Character #___: | Character #___: | Character #___: |
|---|---|---|---|
| What did this character do that was correct? | | | |
| Identify their error | | | |
| What do they need to know to understand for next time? | | | |

118

# TAKING ON THE B.E.S.T.

Rewrite the numeral–word form of the fractions in standard form. Then, find the sum or difference. Include a visual model that represents the expression.

**1** 1 fourth + 3 eighths

**2** 5 sixths – 1 third

**3** 8 twelfths + 1 half

# TAKING ON THE B.E.S.T.

**MA.5.FR.2.1** | **Extra Practice #1** | **Add and Subtract Fractions** (Only Need to Rewrite One Fraction)

Rewrite the numeral–word form of the fractions in standard form. Then, find the sum or difference. Include a visual model that represents the expression.

**1** 1 fifth + 4 tenths

**2** 2 fourths − 1 eighth

**3** 11 twelfths + 4 sixths

# TAKING ON THE B.E.S.T.

 Video Lesson

## Add and Subtract Fractions
(Rewrite both fractions)

Rewrite the numeral–word form of the fractions in standard form. Then, find the sum or difference. Include a visual model that represents the expression.

**1** 2 tenths + 1 third

**2** 7 fifths – 1 fourth

**3** 3 sixths + 5 eighths

121

**MA.5.FR.2.1** | **Extra Practice #2** | **Add and Subtract Fractions** (Rewrite both fractions)

Rewrite the numeral–word form of the fractions in standard form. Then, find the sum or difference. Include a visual model that represents the expression.

**1** 3 twelfths + 2 fifths

**2** 8 tenths – 5 eighths

**3** 4 sixths + 3 fourths

# TAKING ON THE B.E.S.T.

  Video Lesson | **Addition with Fractions Greater Than One**

Find the sum of each expression.

1. $2\frac{4}{5} + 3\frac{1}{6}$

2. $4\frac{7}{8} + 3\frac{3}{4}$

3. $2\frac{1}{2} + 1\frac{1}{6} + 3\frac{8}{12}$

123

# TAKING ON THE B.E.S.T.

| Extra Practice #3 | Addition with Fractions Greater Than One

Find the sum of each expression.

1. $5\frac{1}{5} + 4\frac{1}{2}$

2. $6\frac{6}{10} + 1\frac{2}{4}$

3. $1\frac{2}{3} + 2\frac{4}{6} + 5\frac{1}{12}$

# TAKING ON THE B.E.S.T.

  Video Lesson **Subtraction with Fractions Greater Than One**

Find the difference of each expression.

**1** $2\frac{4}{5} - 1\frac{1}{6}$

**2** $4\frac{5}{8} - 3\frac{3}{4}$

**3** $8\frac{1}{2} - 3\frac{4}{6}$

Find the difference of each expression.

1. $3\frac{7}{8} - 2\frac{1}{3}$

2. $6\frac{2}{12} - 4\frac{3}{5}$

3. $7\frac{1}{3} - \frac{10}{12}$

# TAKING ON THE B.E.S.T.

**Math Missions**

**Add and Subtract Fractions with Unlike Denominators**

Ian records the time he spends writing his book in the table to the right.

| DAY | HOURS SPENT WRITING |
|---|---|
| Monday | $3\frac{5}{8}$ |
| Wednesday | $1\frac{1}{6}$ |
| Thursday | $2\frac{3}{5}$ |
| Sunday | $2\frac{1}{2}$ |

## PART ONE

How many hours does he write on Monday, Thursday, and Sunday combined?

## PART TWO

How many more hours did he write on Thursday than Sunday?

# TAKING ON THE B.E.S.T.

## Math Misconception Mystery
### (PAGE 1)

**BEFORE THE VIDEO:** Solve the problem on your own.

Find the difference: $7\frac{1}{12} - 6\frac{4}{5}$

**DURING THE VIDEO:** Pause after each "character" solves the problem and jot down quick notes to help you remember what they did correctly or incorrectly.

| Character #1 _____ | Character #2 _____ |
|---|---|
| | |
| **Character #3** _____ | **Character #4** _____ |
| | |

# TAKING ON THE B.E.S.T.

## Math Misconception Mystery (PAGE 2)

**AFTER THE VIDEO:** Discuss and analyze their answers.

The most reasonable answer belongs to Character # _____ because

_____

_____

_____

_____

(Justify how this character's work makes sense.)

### Let's help the others:

| | Character #___: | Character #___: | Character #___: |
|---|---|---|---|
| What did this character do that was correct? | | | |
| Identify their error | | | |
| What do they need to know to understand for next time? | | | |

129

# TAKING ON THE B.E.S.T.

MA.5.FR.2.2  Video Lesson | **Multiplying Fractions Less Than One**

Find the product of each expression. Include a visual model and a standard algorithm. Simplify the fractions (if possible) for extra practice.

**1** $\frac{4}{5} \times \frac{2}{3}$

**2** $\frac{3}{8} \times \frac{3}{4}$

**3** Lamar has $\frac{1}{2}$ —cup of sugar. He uses $\frac{1}{4}$ of the sugar for a recipe. How much sugar did he use?

# TAKING ON THE B.E.S.T.

**Extra Practice #1**

**Multiplying Fractions Less Than One**

Find the product of each expression. Include a visual model and a standard algorithm. Simplify the fractions for extra practice.

**1** $\dfrac{6}{10} \times \dfrac{3}{12}$

**2** $\dfrac{5}{6} \times \dfrac{1}{3}$

**3** Lamar has $\dfrac{2}{3}$—cup of sugar. He uses $\dfrac{2}{5}$ of the sugar for a recipe. How much sugar did he use?

# TAKING ON THE B.E.S.T.

  **Video Lesson** | **Multiplying Fractions Greater Than One**

Find the product of each expression. Include a visual model and a standard algorithm. Simplify the fractions for extra practice.

**1** $2\frac{1}{2} \times 3\frac{1}{4}$

**2** $1\frac{1}{3} \times 4\frac{3}{5}$

**3** Janelle purchase $3\frac{1}{4}$ pounds of gravel from the local home improvement store. She uses $\frac{1}{2}$ of the amount of gravel in her driveway. How much of the gravel does she use?

# TAKING ON THE B.E.S.T.

**Extra Practice #2**

## Multiplying Fractions Greater Than One

Find the product of each expression. Include a visual model and a standard algorithm. Simplify the fractions for extra practice.

**1** $1\frac{1}{3} \times 2\frac{1}{5}$

**2** $2\frac{2}{3} \times 2\frac{1}{2}$

**3** Janelle purchase $4\frac{3}{4}$ pounds of gravel from the local home improvement store. She uses $\frac{1}{2}$ of the amount of gravel in her driveway. How much of the gravel does she use?

# TAKING ON THE B.E.S.T.

  Video Lesson | Multiplying Fractions with an Extra Step

1. Joey has $4\frac{3}{8}$ yards of string. He uses a third of the string for a project. How much string does he have left?

2. A painter must paint $10\frac{2}{3}$ feet of wall. So far, he has completed $\frac{2}{3}$ of the the project. How much of the length of wall has he painted? How much more wall length does he have to paint?

# TAKING ON THE B.E.S.T.

**1** Mrs. Hendricks has $3\frac{2}{6}$ gallons of water in a container. She pours $\frac{1}{3}$ of the water down the drain. How much water is in the container now?

**2** A local restaurant cooks $9\frac{3}{4}$ pounds of potatoes for an event. The guests eat $\frac{3}{4}$ of the potatoes. How much of the potatoes were eaten? How much of the potatoes remain?

| MA.5.FR.2.2 | Math Missions | Multiplying Fractions |

Adnan swims $1\frac{4}{5}$ miles each week. His brother, Yusuf, swims $2\frac{1}{3}$ times the distance Adnan swims.

## PART ONE

How far does Yusuf swim?

## PART TWO

How much further does Adnan need to swim to achieve the same distance as Yusuf?

## PART THREE

To figure out how far Yusuf swam, Adnan used the area model. Help Adnan complete the area model, and show how to solve.

|  | $2$ $+$ | $\frac{1}{3}$ |
|---|---|---|
| $1$ $+$ |  | $\frac{1}{3}$ |
| $\frac{4}{5}$ |  | $\frac{4}{15}$ |

# TAKING ON THE B.E.S.T.

## Math Misconception Mystery (PAGE 1)

**BEFORE THE VIDEO:** Solve the problem on your own.

Find the product: $\frac{3}{4}$ x $\frac{3}{4}$

**DURING THE VIDEO:** Pause after each "character" solves the problem and jot down quick notes to help you remember what they did correctly or incorrectly.

| Character #1 _____ | Character #2 _____ |
|---|---|
| | |
| Character #3 _____ | Character #4 _____ |
| | |

# TAKING ON THE B.E.S.T.

**AFTER THE VIDEO:** Discuss and analyze their answers.

The most reasonable answer belongs to Character # _____ because

_____

_____

_____

_____

(Justify how this character's work makes sense.)

## Let's help the others:

| | Character #___: | Character #___: | Character #___: |
|---|---|---|---|
| What did this character do that was correct? | | | |
| Identify their error | | | |
| What do they need to know to understand for next time? | | | |

# TAKING ON THE B.E.S.T.

For each expression, model with a drawing to understand what happens to the product when you multiply $\frac{2}{3}$ by a fraction less than 1, equal to 1, and greater than 1.

**1**    $\frac{2}{3} \times \frac{1}{2}$

**2**    $\frac{2}{3} \times \frac{2}{2}$

**3**    $\frac{2}{3} \times \frac{3}{2}$

# TAKING ON THE B.E.S.T.

**Extra Practice #1**

**How to Predict the Relative Size of a Product - Discover the Rules**

For each expression, model with a drawing to understand what happens to the product when you multiply $\frac{1}{2}$ by a fraction less than 1, equal to 1, and greater than 1.

**1** $\frac{1}{2} \times \frac{1}{2}$

**2** $\frac{1}{2} \times \frac{2}{2}$

**3** $\frac{1}{2} \times \frac{3}{2}$

# TAKING ON THE B.E.S.T.

**MA.5.FR.2.3** |  **Video Lesson** | **Predict the Relative Size of a Product**

For each expression, explain what happens to the product when you multiply $1\frac{2}{3}$ by a fraction less than 1, equal to 1, and greater than 1.

---

**1**   $1\frac{2}{3} \times \frac{3}{4}$

---

**2**   $1\frac{2}{3} \times 1\frac{2}{3}$

---

**3**   $1\frac{2}{3} \times \frac{4}{4}$

# TAKING ON THE B.E.S.T.

**MA.5.FR.2.3** | **Extra Practice #2** | **Predict the Relative Size of a Product**

For each expression, explain what happens to the product when you multiply $2\frac{1}{4}$ by a fraction less than 1, equal to 1, and greater than 1.

**1** $2\frac{1}{4} \times \frac{2}{5}$

**2** $2\frac{1}{4} \times \frac{5}{2}$

**3** $2\frac{1}{4} \times \frac{5}{5}$

# TAKING ON THE B.E.S.T.

**MA.5.FR.2.3** | **Extra Practice #3** | **Predict the Relative Size of a Product**

For each expression, explain what happens to the product when you multiply 4 by a fraction less than 1, equal to 1, and greater than 1.

**1** $4 \times 4\frac{1}{10}$

**2** $4 \times \frac{1}{10}$

**3** $4 \times \frac{10}{10}$

# TAKING ON THE B.E.S.T.

**MA.5.FR.2.3**  **Video Lesson** | **Predict the Relative Size of a Product: Connect to Decimals**

For each expression, explain what happens to the product when you multiply 3 by a value than 1, equal to 1, and greater than 1.

**1**   3 x 1.01

**2**   3 x 0.99

**3**   3 x 1.00

# TAKING ON THE B.E.S.T.

**MA.5.FR.2.3** | **Extra Practice #4** | **Predict the Relative Size of a Product: Connect to Decimals**

For each expression, explain what happens to the product when you multiply 2 by a value than 1, equal to 1, and greater than 1.

**1** 2 x 1.0

**2** 2 x 0.75

**3** 2 x 1.37

# TAKING ON THE B.E.S.T.

| MA.5.FR.2.3 | Math Missions | Predict the Relative Size of a Product |

Rachel is playing a game. She currently has 14,328 points.

## PART ONE

Rachel has to multiply her point value by a factor that will increase her points. Some options are provided below. Select all the possible options that would increase her point value. Explain your answer on the lines below.

| $1\frac{2}{7}$ | $\frac{99}{100}$ | 1.86 | $\frac{991}{991}$ | $\frac{5}{6}$ | 0.01 |

_____

_____

_____

_____

_____

## PART TWO

For the next round, Rachel must select all the possible options that would keep her point value the same. Rachel's cousin, Jeremy, looks at the same options, and says, "There is no way to accomplish this!"

Do you agree or disagree with Jeremy? Explain your thinking on the lines below.

_____

_____

_____

_____

# TAKING ON THE B.E.S.T.

| **Math Misconception Mystery (PAGE 1)**

**BEFORE THE VIDEO:** Solve the problem on your own.

Which of the following expressions will have a product less than 5?

Ⓐ $\frac{7}{8} \times 5$

Ⓑ $5 \times \frac{98}{89}$

Ⓒ $5 \times \frac{100}{100}$

Ⓓ $1\frac{1}{8} \times 5$

**DURING THE VIDEO:** Pause after each "character" solves the problem and jot down quick notes to help you remember what they did correctly or incorrectly.

Character #1 _____

Character #2 _____

Character #3 _____

Character #4 _____

**MA.5.FR.2.3**

## Math Misconception Mystery (PAGE 2)

**AFTER THE VIDEO:** Discuss and analyze their answers.

The most reasonable answer belongs to Character # _____ because

_____

_____

_____

_____

(Justify how this character's work makes sense.)

## Let's help the others:

|  | Character #___: | Character #___: | Character #___: |
|---|---|---|---|
| What did this character do that was correct? |  |  |  |
| Identify their error |  |  |  |
| What do they need to know to understand for next time? |  |  |  |

148

# TAKING ON THE B.E.S.T.

**MA.5.FR.2.4**  Video Lesson **Divide Whole Numbers by a Unit Fraction**

For each expression, model with an area model and number line to solve.

**1** $4 \div \dfrac{1}{2}$

**2** $2 \div \dfrac{1}{3}$

**3** $3 \div \dfrac{1}{4}$

# TAKING ON THE B.E.S.T.

**MA.5.FR.2.4** | **Extra Practice #1** | **Divide Whole Numbers by a Unit Fraction**

For each expression, model with an area model and number line to solve.

**1** $5 \div \dfrac{1}{3}$

**2** $4 \div \dfrac{1}{4}$

**3** $10 \div \dfrac{1}{2}$

# TAKING ON THE B.E.S.T.

**MA.5.FR.2.4** |  Video Lesson | **Divide a Unit Fraction by a Whole Number**

For each expression, model with an area model and number line to solve.

**1** $\frac{1}{2} \div 4$

**2** $\frac{1}{3} \div 2$

**3** $\frac{1}{4} \div 3$

# TAKING ON THE B.E.S.T.

**MA.5.FR.2.4** | **Extra Practice #2** | **Divide a Unit Fraction by a Whole Number**

For each expression, model with an area model and number line to solve.

**1** $\frac{1}{3} \div 5$

**2** $\frac{1}{4} \div 4$

**3** $\frac{1}{2} \div 10$

**1** Karina runs in a 5 mile race. She takes a brief water break at every $\frac{1}{3}$ mile. How many times does she stop to take a water break during the race?

**2** Sam bakes a pan of brownies. After a party, $\frac{1}{5}$ of the original pan of brownies remains. Sam shares the remaining brownie equally onto three plates. How much of the original brownie is on each plate?

# TAKING ON THE B.E.S.T.

**1** Karina runs in a 6 mile race. She takes a brief water break at every $\frac{1}{4}$ mile. How many times does she stop to take a water break during the race?

**2** Sam bakes a pan of brownies. After a party, $\frac{1}{3}$ of the original pan of brownies remains. Sam shares the remaining brownie equally onto seven plates. How much of the original brownie is on each plate?

# TAKING ON THE B.E.S.T.

| MA.5.FR.2.4 | Math Missions | Division with Unit Fractions |
| --- | --- | --- |

Maleek's mom orders four pizzas for his birthday party.

## PART ONE

If each whole pizza is cut into fourths, how many slices will be available? Include a visual model to represent your thinking.

## PART TWO

If each whole pizza is cut into eighths, how many slices will be available? Include a visual model to represent your thinking.

## PART THREE

There will be 16 people at Maleek's party. Which slicing option would be the best – cut into fourths or eighths? Explain your thinking on the lines below.

_____

_____

_____

_____

# TAKING ON THE B.E.S.T.

## MA.5.FR.2.4 | Math Misconception Mystery (PAGE 1)

**BEFORE THE VIDEO:** Solve the problem on your own.

> What is the quotient of $\frac{1}{6} \div 8$? Include a visual model to represent your thinking.

**DURING THE VIDEO:** Pause after each "character" solves the problem and jot down quick notes to help you remember what they did correctly or incorrectly.

| Character #1 _____ | Character #2 _____ |
|---|---|
| | |
| **Character #3** _____ | **Character #4** _____ |
| | |

# TAKING ON THE B.E.S.T.

| MA.5.FR.2.4 | Math Misconception Mystery (PAGE 2) |

**AFTER THE VIDEO:** Discuss and analyze their answers.

The most reasonable answer belongs to Character # _____ because

_____

_____

_____

_____

(Justify how this character's work makes sense.)

## Let's help the others:

|  | Character #___: | Character #___: | Character #___: |
|---|---|---|---|
| What did this character do that was correct? |  |  |  |
| Identify their error |  |  |  |
| What do they need to know to understand for next time? |  |  |  |

# TAKING ON THE B.E.S.T.

**1** Dave buys 14 packages of markers for $9 each. Then, he purchases 17 cases of water for $11 each. How much more did he spend on water than on markers?

**2** Yoshi has 1,287 stickers. His dad gives him 1,058 stickers for his birthday. Yoshi places 25 stickers on each page in his sticker binder. How many pages will he need to hold his stickers?

**1** There are 900 students at Lakeshore Elementary. The students in 3rd, 4th, and 5th grade are going on a field trip, leaving behind 388 students. The students who are going on the field trip will be able to fit 37 students on each bus. How many buses will be needed to transport all of the students?

**2** Kyle delivers cases of paper with 24 reams in each case. On Monday, he delivers 128 cases of paper. On Tuesday, Kyle delivers 135 cases of paper. How many more reams of paper does Kyle deliver on Tuesday?

# TAKING ON THE B.E.S.T.

The students at Franklin Academy collect gallons of water to deliver to their local food bank. The table shows the number of gallons each grade collects.

| Grade | Gallons of Water |
|-------|------------------|
| K | 24 |
| 1 | 35 |
| 2 | 47 |
| 3 | 55 |
| 4 | 67 |
| 5 | 78 |

## PART ONE

If each gallon of water is equivalent to 16 cups, how many total cups of water did the students at Franklin Academy collect?

## PART TWO

If each gallon of water is equivalent to 4 quarts, how many more quarts of water does 5th grade collect compared to Kindergarten and 1st grade combined?

160

# TAKING ON THE B.E.S.T.

## Math Misconception Mystery
### (PAGE I)

**BEFORE THE VIDEO:** Solve the problem on your own.

An orange juice factory receives 54 crates of oranges in the morning and 49 crates in the afternoon. Each crate of oranges is 25 pounds. It takes 13 pounds of oranges to make a gallon of orange juice. How many gallons of orange juice can be made with today's delivery?

**DURING THE VIDEO:** Pause after each "character" solves the problem and jot down quick notes to help you remember what they did correctly or incorrectly.

Character #1 _____

Character #2 _____

Character #3 _____

Character #4 _____

161

# TAKING ON THE B.E.S.T.

**MA.5.AR.1.1** | ## Math Misconception Mystery (PAGE 2)

**AFTER THE VIDEO:** Discuss and analyze their answers.

The most reasonable answer belongs to Character # _____ because

_____

_____

_____

_____

(Justify how this character's work makes sense.)

### Let's help the others:

|  | Character #___: | Character #___: | Character #___: |
|---|---|---|---|
| What did this character do that was correct? |  |  |  |
| Identify their error |  |  |  |
| What do they need to know to understand for next time? |  |  |  |

Nick has $1\frac{1}{3}$ gallons of water.

He purchases another 3 gallons from the store. How much water does he have now?

Nick uses $\frac{1}{2}$ of the water for recipe. How much water is needed for the recipe?

With the remaining water, Nick drinks $\frac{1}{8}$ gallon of water. How much water is left?

Charlie works on a house project for $2\frac{2}{3}$ hours on Saturday and $3\frac{3}{4}$ hours on Sunday. How much time did Charlie spend on her house project?

Charlie spent $\frac{2}{5}$ of the time painting and $\frac{1}{5}$ of the time sanding wood. How much time Charlie spend on each task?

Next weekend, Charlie wants to spend 10 hours working on a house project. How much more time does she want to spend next weekend compared to this weekend?

Mrs. Simpkins graded papers for $4\frac{1}{6}$ hours last week. This week, she cuts down on her grading time by $1\frac{1}{2}$ hours. How much time does she spend grading papers this week?

This week, Mrs. Simpkins listens to classical music while grading papers, but only for $\frac{2}{3}$ of the time. How much time does she spend listening to classical music?

The following week, Mrs. Simpkins only grades papers for $\frac{2}{3}$ hour. How much time did she spend grading papers if she combines the times for the three weeks?

# TAKING ON THE B.E.S.T.

| MA.5.AR.I.2 | Math Missions | Add, Subtract, and Multiply Fractions and Mixed Numbers (Real World Problems) |
|---|---|---|

Create real-world problems for each of the expressions.

**PART ONE** $1\frac{3}{8} + \frac{4}{6}$

**PART TWO** $1\frac{3}{8} - \frac{4}{6}$

**PART THREE** $1\frac{3}{8} \times \frac{4}{6}$

# TAKING ON THE B.E.S.T.

## Math Misconception Mystery
## (PAGE 1)

**BEFORE THE VIDEO:** Solve the problem on your own.

Monique has $1\frac{3}{4}$ cups of sugar. She uses $\frac{2}{3}$ of the sugar for a recipe for strawberry shortcake. After she makes the strawberry shortcake, how much sugar is left?

**DURING THE VIDEO:** Pause after each "character" solves the problem and jot down quick notes to help you remember what they did correctly or incorrectly.

Character #1 _____

Character #2 _____

Character #3 _____

Character #4 _____

# TAKING ON THE B.E.S.T.

**Math Misconception Mystery (PAGE 2)**

**AFTER THE VIDEO:** Discuss and analyze their answers.

The most reasonable answer belongs to Character # _____ because

_____

_____

_____

_____

(Justify how this character's work makes sense.)

## Let's help the others:

|  | Character #___: | Character #___: | Character #___: |
|---|---|---|---|
| What did this character do that was correct? |  |  |  |
| Identify their error |  |  |  |
| What do they need to know to understand for next time? |  |  |  |

# TAKING ON THE B.E.S.T.

  Video Lesson | **Division with Unit Fractions (Real World Problems)**

**1** Jonathan has 5 gallons of water. His water bottle holds $\frac{1}{4}$ gallons of water. How many times can Jonathan fill his water bottle?

**2** Mr. Turner spends $\frac{1}{2}$ hour grading math tests. In this time, he is able to grade 10 tests. If he spends an equal amount of time grading each test, how long does it him to grade one test?

# TAKING ON THE B.E.S.T.

**1** Aaron has $\frac{1}{3}$ of an apple pie leftover from a party. He slices the pie into 2 equal pieces to share with a friend. How much of the original pie does each person get?

**2** Aaron makes 2 apple pies. He cuts each pie, so that each slice represents $\frac{1}{3}$ of a pie. How many total slices of apple pie does Aaron make?

# TAKING ON THE B.E.S.T.

**1** Zach orders 6 pizzas. Each slice is $\frac{1}{8}$ of the pizza. How many slices are there altogether?

**2** Eduardo bakes a batch of brownies. After he shares the brownies at a family gathering, $\frac{1}{6}$ of the pan is left. He cuts the remaining brownies into 3 equal pieces. How much of the original pan is each piece?

# TAKING ON THE B.E.S.T.

| MA.5.AR.I.3 | Math Missions | Division with Unit Fractions (Real World Problems) |
|---|---|---|

## PART ONE

Create a real-world scenario for the expression: $\frac{1}{4} \div 3$

Include a visual representation and solve.

## PART TWO

Create a real-world scenario for the expression: $3 \div \frac{1}{4}$

Include a visual representation and solve.

# TAKING ON THE B.E.S.T.

## Math Misconception Mystery
### (PAGE I)

**BEFORE THE VIDEO:** Solve the problem on your own.

> Eliza has 12 yards of ribbon. She uses $\frac{1}{3}$ yard of ribbon to wrap each present. How many presents can she wrap in all?

**DURING THE VIDEO:** Pause after each "character" solves the problem and jot down quick notes to help you remember what they did correctly or incorrectly.

| Character #1 _____ | Character #2 _____ |
|---|---|
| | |
| **Character #3** _____ | **Character #4** _____ |
| | |

# TAKING ON THE B.E.S.T.

## Math Misconception Mystery (PAGE 2)

**AFTER THE VIDEO:** Discuss and analyze their answers.

The most reasonable answer belongs to Character # _____ because

_____

_____

_____

_____

(Justify how this character's work makes sense.)

### Let's help the others:

| | Character #___: | Character #___: | Character #___: |
|---|---|---|---|
| What did this character do that was correct? | | | |
| Identify their error | | | |
| What do they need to know to understand for next time? | | | |

# TAKING ON THE B.E.S.T.

  Video Lesson | **Numerical Expressions into Mathematical Descriptions**

Interpret each numerical expression into at least two different mathematical descriptions.

**1** $4 \times (6 + 2)$

**2** $\frac{1}{2} \times (100 - 58)$

**3** $(6 \times 8) - (12.5 + 8.04)$

# TAKING ON THE B.E.S.T.

Interpret each numerical expression into at least two different mathematical descriptions.

**1** $9 \div (11 - 8)$

**2** $\frac{1}{3} \times (88 - 76)$

**3** $(15.2 \div 3.8) + (11.18 \times 2.1)$

176

# TAKING ON THE B.E.S.T.

  **Video Lesson** | **Mathematical Descriptions into Numerical Expressions**

Interpret each mathematical description as a numerical expression.

**1** The quantity of two and two hundredths plus four and five tenths multiplied by three.

**2** Half the sum of six and four, minus one and thirteen hundredths.

**3** The product of nine and four plus the difference of ten from twenty.

# TAKING ON THE B.E.S.T.

Interpret each mathematical description as a numerical expression.

**1** The quantity of four and two tenths minus one and nine hundredths added to twelve.

**2** Half the difference of twenty from forty-two, plus three and thirty-one hundredths.

**3** The quotient of twenty-four and six plus the difference of three and two tenths from fifteen.

# TAKING ON THE B.E.S.T.

**MA.5.AR.2.1** | **Math Missions** | **Interpreting Numerical Expressions and Mathematical Descriptions**

### PART ONE

Francesca says the numerical expression "(4 + 2) x (15 ÷ 5)" can be written as "the quantity of four plus two multiplied by the product of fifteen and five." Explain Francesca's error. Then, write the mathematical description correctly.

_____

_____

_____

_____

_____

### PART TWO

Fill in the blanks with values of your own. Then write a correct numerical expression to match the mathematical description.

$$\boxed{\phantom{0}} \times \left( \boxed{\phantom{0}} + \boxed{\phantom{0}} \right)$$

_____

_____

_____

_____

# TAKING ON THE B.E.S.T.

## Math Misconception Mystery
### (PAGE 1)

**BEFORE THE VIDEO:** Solve the problem on your own.

> Translate the numerical expression below into a written mathematical description.
>
> $$3(42.8 \div 4)$$

**DURING THE VIDEO:** Pause after each "character" solves the problem and jot down quick notes to help you remember what they did correctly or incorrectly.

| Character #1 _____ | Character #2 _____ |
|---|---|
|  |  |
| Character #3 _____ | Character #4 _____ |
|  |  |

# TAKING ON THE B.E.S.T.

## MA.5.AR.2.1 | Math Misconception Mystery (PAGE 2)

**AFTER THE VIDEO:** Discuss and analyze their answers.

The most reasonable answer belongs to Character # _____ because

_____

_____

_____

_____

(Justify how this character's work makes sense.)

### Let's help the others:

| | Character #___: | Character #___: | Character #___: |
|---|---|---|---|
| What did this character do that was correct? | | | |
| Identify their error | | | |
| What do they need to know to understand for next time? | | | |

181

# TAKING ON THE B.E.S.T.

**MA.5.AR.2.2**  **Video Lesson** | **How to Evaluate Numerical Expressions**

What do you notice about the two expressions below? How do you think you should go about solving them?

$$3 + 2 \times 4 \qquad\qquad 3 \times 2 + 4$$

Let me introduce you to P.E.M.D.A.S!

| | |
|---|---|
| | |
| | |
| | |

Explain why the implementation of the Order of Operations is important.

_____

_____

_____

_____

# TAKING ON THE B.E.S.T.

 Video Lesson

Evaluate Basic Numerical Expressions

Evaluate each numerical expression using the Order of Operations.

**1** (16 ÷ 4) x (10 − 6)

**2** (16 ÷ 4) x 10 − 6

**3** 16 ÷ 4 x (10 − 6)

183

# TAKING ON THE B.E.S.T.

**Extra Practice #1**

**Evaluate Basic Numerical Expressions**

Evaluate each numerical expression using the Order of Operations.

**1** $14 + 15 - 8 \times 0$

**2** $(14 + 15 - 8) \times 0$

**3** $(14 + 15) - (8 + 0)$

Evaluate each numerical expression using the Order of Operations.

**1** $\frac{1}{2} \times (100 \div 5) - 8.5$

**2** $(\frac{1}{2} \times 100) \div 5 - 8.5$

**3** $\frac{1}{2} \times 100 \div 5 - 8.5$

# TAKING ON THE B.E.S.T.

MA.5.AR.2.2 | Extra Practice #2 | **Evaluate More Complex Numerical Expressions**

Evaluate each numerical expression using the Order of Operations.

**1** (185 − 23.34 + 7.66) x 3.2

**2** 185 − 23.34 + 7.66 x 3.2

**3** 185 − (23.34 + 7.66) x 3.2

# TAKING ON THE B.E.S.T.

**MA.5.AR.2.2** | **Math Missions** | **Evaluate Numerical Expressions**

## PART ONE

Insert one set of parentheses to make the expression true. Explain your thinking on the lines below.

$$8 + 8 \times 8 - 8 \div 8 = 15$$

_____

_____

_____

_____

_____

## PART TWO

Insert one set of parentheses around a different pair of numbers. Then evaluate this expression. Explain why the value changed on the lines below.

$$8 + 8 \times 8 - 8 \div 8$$

_____

_____

_____

_____

_____

# TAKING ON THE B.E.S.T.

**Math Misconception Mystery (PAGE 1)**

**BEFORE THE VIDEO:** Solve the problem on your own.

> What is the value of the numerical expression below?
>
> $$3(42.8 \div 4) - 8.5 \times 2.1$$

**DURING THE VIDEO:** Pause after each "character" solves the problem and jot down quick notes to help you remember what they did correctly or incorrectly.

| Character #1 _____ | Character #2 _____ |
|---|---|
| | |
| **Character #3** _____ | **Character #4** _____ |
| | |

# TAKING ON THE B.E.S.T.

**Math Misconception Mystery (PAGE 2)**

**AFTER THE VIDEO:** Discuss and analyze their answers.

The most reasonable answer belongs to Character # _____ because

_____

_____

_____

_____

(Justify how this character's work makes sense.)

## Let's help the others:

|  | Character #___: | Character #___: | Character #___: |
|---|---|---|---|
| What did this character do that was correct? |  |  |  |
| Identify their error |  |  |  |
| What do they need to know to understand for next time? |  |  |  |

189

# TAKING ON THE B.E.S.T.

  **Video Lesson** | **True or False Equations**

Determine and explain whether each equation is true or false.

**1** $5.5 + (12 \times 8) = 203 \div 2$

**2** $100 - 5 + 3 \times 3.2 = 308.16 + 5.44$

**3** $\frac{1}{2}(100 \div 5) + 12 = 5 \times 5.5 - 7.5$

190

# TAKING ON THE B.E.S.T.

| Extra Practice | **True or False Equations**

Determine and explain whether each equation is true or false.

**1** $16 \times (30.8 - 9.88) = 329.15 + 5.57$

**2** $12 \times 12 + 12 \div 12 = 12 \times (12 + 12) \div 12$

**3** $\frac{1}{3}(75 \times 5) + 2.08 = 508.32 \div 4$

# TAKING ON THE B.E.S.T.

**MA.5.AR.2.3** | **Math Missions** | **True or False Equations**

## PART ONE

Use the cards below to create an equation that is true. Explain how you know it's true.

**CARDS**

| 3 | 6.86 | 12 |
| --- | --- | --- |
| 18 | 69.42 | |

$$\left( \Box + \Box \right) - \Box = \Box \div \Box$$

_____

_____

_____

_____

_____

## PART TWO

Use the same cards to create an equation that is false. Explain how you know it is false.

_____

_____

_____

_____

192

# TAKING ON THE B.E.S.T.

## MA.5.AR.2.3 | Math Misconception Mystery (PAGE 1)

**BEFORE THE VIDEO:** Solve the problem on your own.

> Determine if the equation is true or false.
>
> $$4(13.8 \div 2) = 30 - 2.4$$

**DURING THE VIDEO:** Pause after each "character" solves the problem and jot down quick notes to help you remember what they did correctly or incorrectly.

| Character #1 _____ | Character #2 _____ |
|---|---|
| | |
| **Character #3** _____ | **Character #4** _____ |
| | |

193

# TAKING ON THE B.E.S.T.

**Math Misconception Mystery (PAGE 2)**

**AFTER THE VIDEO:** Discuss and analyze their answers.

The most reasonable answer belongs to Character # _____ because

_____

_____

_____

_____

(Justify how this character's work makes sense.)

## Let's help the others:

|  | Character #___: | Character #___: | Character #___: |
|---|---|---|---|
| What did this character do that was correct? |  |  |  |
| Identify their error |  |  |  |
| What do they need to know to understand for next time? |  |  |  |

Patrick has $100 in his savings account. He earns the same amount of money each week for bringing his neighbors' trash cans down to the curb and back. He decides to save all of his money. After six weeks, he has a total of $142.

Create an equation based on the scenario. Use $m$ to represent the amount of money Patrick earns each week.

Then, justify how your equation is correct by checking your solution for $m$.

# TAKING ON THE B.E.S.T.

| **Extra Practice #1** | **Create Equations for Real-World Problems**

Kourtney is creating goodie bags for her party. There are four first graders and eighteen fifth graders coming to her party. She wants each child to receive a goodie bag, and each bag will have the same number of erasers in it. She purchases 66 erasers.

Create an equation based on the scenario. Use *e* to represent the number of erasers Kourtney places in each goodie bag.

Then, justify how your equation is correct by checking your solution for *e*.

| MA.5.AR.2.4 | Extra Practice #2 | Create Equations for Real-World Problems |
|---|---|---|

Mrs. Rose picked 23 flowers in her garden. She placed some of the flowers in her vase. She took half of the remaining flowers to her friend, Betsy, and left the rest for a project.

Create an equation based on the scenario. Use $V$ to represent the number of flowers Mrs. Rose keeps in her vase.

Then, justify how your equation is correct by checking your solution for $V$.

# TAKING ON THE B.E.S.T.

**MA.5.AR.2.4** | **Math Missions** | **Equations Based on Real-World Problems**

## PART ONE

Create a real-world problem based on the equation below.

$$40 - (6 \times N) = 16$$

_____

_____

_____

_____

_____

_____

## PART TWO

What is the value of the $N$? Explain how you know on the lines below.

_____

_____

_____

_____

_____

# TAKING ON THE B.E.S.T.

## Math Misconception Mystery (PAGE 1)

**BEFORE THE VIDEO:** Solve the problem on your own.

> Muriel goes to the grocery store with some money in her wallet. At the store, she purchases three gallons of milk for $4 each. She also purchases four boxes of cereal, for $5 each. She receives $33 in change.
>
> Create an equation to show how much money, **M**, Muriel had in her wallet when she entered the grocery store.

**DURING THE VIDEO:** Pause after each "character" solves the problem and jot down quick notes to help you remember what they did correctly or incorrectly.

| Character #1 _____ | Character #2 _____ |
|---|---|
| | |
| **Character #3** _____ | **Character #4** _____ |
| | |

# TAKING ON THE B.E.S.T.

**Math Misconception Mystery (PAGE 2)**

**AFTER THE VIDEO:** Discuss and analyze their answers.

The most reasonable answer belongs to Character # _____ because

_____

_____

_____

_____

(Justify how this character's work makes sense.)

## Let's help the others:

|  | Character #___: | Character #___: | Character #___: |
|---|---|---|---|
| What did this character do that was correct? |  |  |  |
| Identify their error |  |  |  |
| What do they need to know to understand for next time? |  |  |  |

200

# TAKING ON THE B.E.S.T.

**MA.5.AR.3.1**  **Video Lesson** | **Writing Rules of Increasing Patterns as Expressions**

For each numerical pattern given, identify and write a rule that can describe the patterns as an expression. Then, find the value of the future term provided.

---

**1** 5, 10, 15, 20,....

Write the rule as an expression.

What is the value of the 9th term?

---

**2** 6, 9, 12, 15, ...

Write the rule as an expression.

What is the value of the 8th term?

---

**3** 10, 14, 18, 22, ...

Write the rule as an expression.

What is the value of the 15th term?

# TAKING ON THE B.E.S.T.

For each numerical pattern given, identify and write a rule that can describe the patterns as an expression. Then, find the value of the future term provided.

---

**1** 2, 4, 6, 8,....

Write the rule as an expression.

What is the value of the 10th term?

---

**2** 0, 4, 8, 12, ...

Write the rule as an expression.

What is the value of the 11th term?

---

**3** 12, 24, 36, 48, ...

Write the rule as an expression.

What is the value of the 12th term?

For each numerical pattern given, identify and write a rule that can describe the patterns as an expression. Then, find the value of the future term provided.

**1** 100, 90, 80, 70, ...

Write the rule as an expression.

What is the value of the 5th term?

**2** 20, 19, 18, 17, ...

Write the rule as an expression.

What is the value of the 8th term?

**3** 45, 40, 35, 30, ...

Write the rule as an expression.

What is the value of the 7th term?

**MA.5.AR.3.1** | **Extra Practice #2** | **Writing Rules of Decreasing Patterns as Expressions**

For each numerical pattern given, identify and write a rule that can describe the patterns as an expression. Then, find the value of the future term provided.

**1** 100, 95, 90, 85, …

Write the rule as an expression.

What is the value of the 10th term?

**2** 32, 30, 28, 26, …

Write the rule as an expression.

What is the value of the 8th term?

**3** 97, 91, 85, 79, …

Write the rule as an expression.

What is the value of the 11th term?

**MA.5.AR.3.1** | **Math Missions** | **Writing Rules of Patterns as Expressions**

## PART ONE

Three rectangles are shown below. Determine the perimeter and area for each.

1 cm ▢
1 cm

1 cm ▭
2 cm

1 cm ▭
3 cm

## PART TWO

Imagine that the pattern continued with the length increasing by 1 centimeter for each rectangle. Describe the pattern of the perimeter using an expression.

_____

_____

Describe the pattern of the area using an expression.

_____

_____

What would be the perimeter and area of the 15th rectangle in the pattern?

_____

_____

**MA.5.AR.3.1** | ## Math Misconception Mystery (PAGE 1)

**BEFORE THE VIDEO:** Solve the problem on your own.

> Write an expression that can be a rule for terms shown below.
>
> 13, 23, 33, ...

**DURING THE VIDEO:** Pause after each "character" solves the problem and jot down quick notes to help you remember what they did correctly or incorrectly.

| Character #1 _____ | Character #2 _____ |
|---|---|
| | |
| Character #3 _____ | Character #4 _____ |
| | |

# TAKING ON THE B.E.S.T.

## Math Misconception Mystery (PAGE 2)

**AFTER THE VIDEO:** Discuss and analyze their answers.

The most reasonable answer belongs to Character # _____ because

_____

_____

_____

_____

(Justify how this character's work makes sense.)

### Let's help the others:

|  | Character #___: | Character #___: | Character #___: |
|---|---|---|---|
| What did this character do that was correct? |  |  |  |
| Identify their error |  |  |  |
| What do they need to know to understand for next time? |  |  |  |

# TAKING ON THE B.E.S.T.

**1** What are the missing values in the table below?

Rule: 23 + 2x

| Input (x) | 0 | 1 | 2 | 3 |
|---|---|---|---|---|
| Output | | 25 | 27 | |

**2** What are the missing values in the table below?

Rule: 75 – 3x

| Input (x) | 0 | 1 | 2 | 3 |
|---|---|---|---|---|
| Output | 75 | 72 | | |

208

**1** What are the missing values in the table below?

Rule: 15 + 3x

| Input (x) | 0 | 1 | 2 | 3 |
|-----------|---|---|---|---|
| Output | 15 | 18 | | |

**2** What are the missing values in the table below?

Rule: 50 – 2x

| Input (x) | 0 | 1 | 2 | 3 |
|-----------|---|---|---|---|
| Output | | 48 | | 44 |

**MA.5.AR.3.2** |  **Video Lesson** | **Graphing Inputs and Outputs as Ordered Pairs**

Fill in the outputs in the table. Create the ordered pairs. Then, plot the points on the coordinate plane below.

Rule: 1 + 2x

| Input (x) | Output | Ordered Pair |
|---|---|---|
| 0 | | |
| 1 | | |
| 2 | | |
| 3 | | |

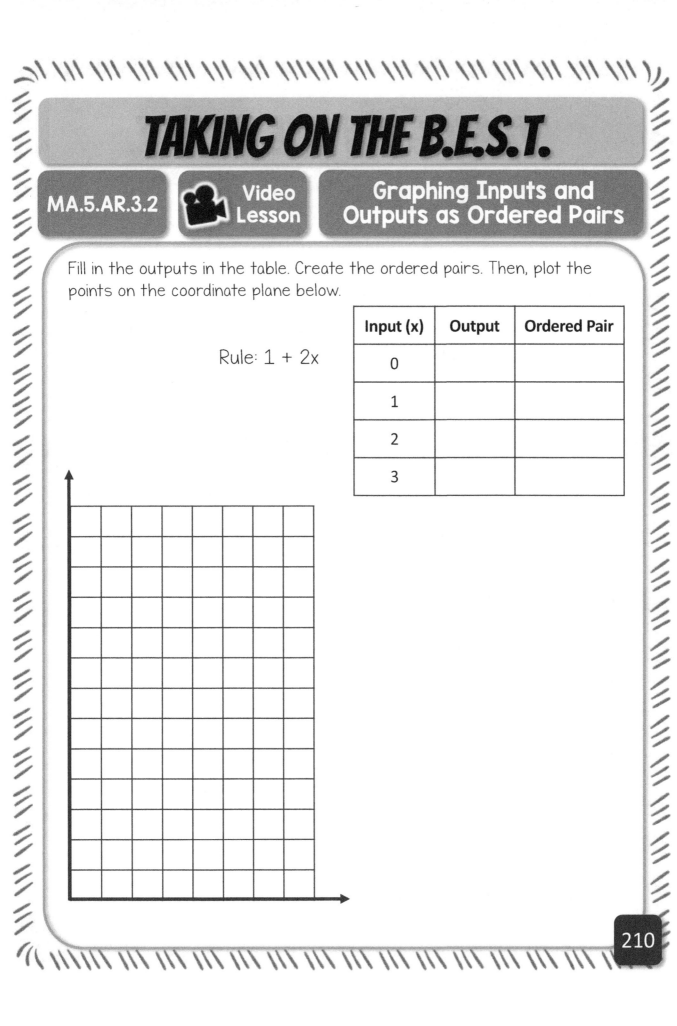

# TAKING ON THE B.E.S.T.

| MA.5.AR.3.2 | Extra Practice #2 | Graphing Inputs and Outputs as Ordered Pairs |

Fill in the outputs in the table. Create the ordered pairs. Then, plot the points on the coordinate plane below.

Rule: 13 – 3x

| Input (x) | Output | Ordered Pair |
|-----------|--------|--------------|
| 0 | | |
| 1 | | |
| 2 | | |
| 3 | | |

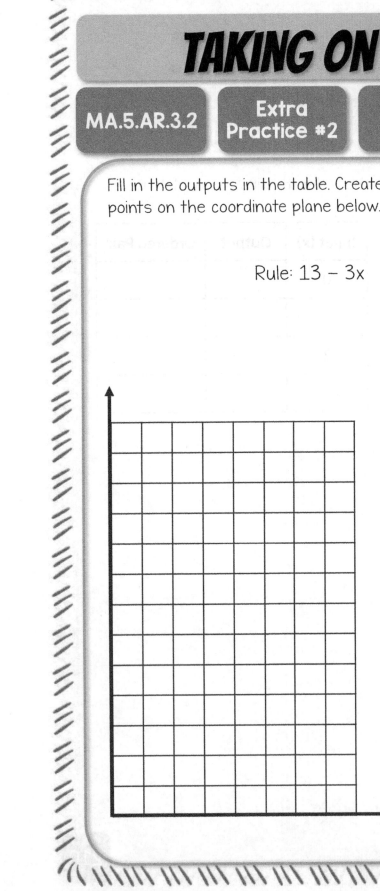

# TAKING ON THE B.E.S.T.

| MA.5.AR.3.2 | Math Missions | Patterns with Inputs and Outputs |
|---|---|---|

## PART ONE

Janie creates an input and output table using the rule, "4 + 3x." Janie makes some mistakes.. Identify which output values are incorrect and replace them with the correct values

| Input (x) | 0 | 1 | 2 | 3 |
|---|---|---|---|---|
| Output | 7 | 7 | 10 | 10 |

## PART TWO

Extend the table to show the outputs for x = 8, 9, and 10.

| MA.5.AR.3.2 | Math Misconception Mystery (PAGE 1) |

**BEFORE THE VIDEO:** Solve the problem on your own.

What are the missing values in the table below?

Rule:
49 - 3x

| Input (x) | 0 | 1 | 2 | 3 |
|---|---|---|---|---|
| Output | | | | |

**DURING THE VIDEO:** Pause after each "character" solves the problem and jot down quick notes to help you remember what they did correctly or incorrectly.

Character #1 _____

Character #2 _____

Character #3 _____

Character #4 _____

# TAKING ON THE B.E.S.T.

## Math Misconception Mystery
### (PAGE 2)

**AFTER THE VIDEO:** Discuss and analyze their answers.

The most reasonable answer belongs to Character # _____ because

_____

_____

_____

_____

(Justify how this character's work makes sense.)

### Let's help the others:

|  | Character #___: | Character #___: | Character #___: |
|---|---|---|---|
| What did this character do that was correct? |  |  |  |
| Identify their error |  |  |  |
| What do they need to know to understand for next time? |  |  |  |

# TAKING ON THE B.E.S.T.

**1** Eugene has 24.5 yards of of string. How many inches of string does Eugene have?

> 1 foot = 12 inches
> 1 yard = 3 feet
> 1 mile = 5,280 feet
> 1 mile = 1,760 yards

**2** Alexa walks 4,500 meters. How many kilometers does Alexa walk? How many centimeters does she walk?

> 1 centimeter = 10 millimeters
> 1 meter = 100 centimeters
> 1 meter = 1000 millimeters
> 1 kilometer = 1000 meters

**MA.5.M.1.1** | **Extra Practice #1** | **Measurement Conversions: Length**

**1** How many yards are in $4\frac{3}{4}$ miles? How many feet are in $4\frac{3}{4}$ miles?

1 foot = 12 inches
1 yard = 3 feet
1 mile = 5,280 feet
1 mile = 1,760 yards

**2** How many millimeters are in 5.75 meters?

1 centimeter = 10 millimeters
1 meter = 100 centimeters
1 meter = 1000 millimeters
1 kilometer = 1000 meters

# TAKING ON THE B.E.S.T.

  Video Lesson | **Measurement Conversions: Capacity (Liquid Volume)**

**1** Katie has 10 quarts of orange juice. How many gallons of orange juice does Katie have? How many fluid ounces of orange juice does Katie have?

> 1 cup = 8 fluid ounces
> 1 pint = 2 cups
> 1 quart = 2 pints
> 1 gallon = 4 quarts

**2** Daqwan has 70,670 milliliters of water. How many liters of water does Daqwan have?

> 1 liter = 1000 milliliters

| MA.5.M.I.I | Extra Practice #2 | Measurement Conversions: Capacity (Liquid Volume) |

**1** Bethany has 22 pints of oil. How many gallons of oil is this? How many fluid ounces of oil does Bethany have?

1 cup = 8 fluid ounces
1 pint = 2 cups
1 quart = 2 pints
1 gallon = 4 quarts

**2** Ricardo's mom asks him to pick up three half-liters of juice from the store. How many milliliters of juice should Ricardo pick up?

1 liter = 1000 milliliters

# TAKING ON THE B.E.S.T.

  Video Lesson | **Measurement Conversions: Weight and Mass**

**1** The Jackson's car has a weight of 7,500 pounds. What is the weight of the car in tons? What is the weight in ounces?

> 1 pound = 16 ounces
> 1 ton = 2,000 pounds

**2** Marty's dog has a mass of $4\frac{9}{10}$ kilograms. Carly's cat has a mass of 3,456 grams. How many more grams is the mass of Marty's dog?

> 1 gram = 1000 milligrams
> 1 kilograms = 1000 grams

219

# TAKING ON THE B.E.S.T.

**1** An elephant weighs 4 tons, 400 pounds. How much does an elephant weigh in ounces?

> 1 pound = 16 ounces
> 1 ton = 2,000 pounds

**2** Freddy's older cat has a mass of $3\frac{1}{2}$ kilograms. His younger cat has a mass of 2,319 grams. What is the total mass of both cats?

> 1 gram = 1000 milligrams
> 1 kilograms = 1000 grams

**1** It takes Dawson 3.5 days to read a book. How many minutes passed by during his time reading the book? How many seconds passed by?

1 minute = 60 seconds
1 hour = 60 minutes
1 day = 24 hours
1 week = 7 days

**2** Jonas is 49 weeks old. How many days old is Jonas? How many hours old is Jonas?

1 minute = 60 seconds
1 hour = 60 minutes
1 day = 24 hours
1 week = 7 days

# TAKING ON THE B.E.S.T.

**1** Marie runs a marathon in 5.5 hours. She set a goal to run in less than 20,000 seconds. Did she achieve her goal? Explain your thinking.

1 minute = 60 seconds
1 hour = 60 minutes
1 day = 24 hours
1 week = 7 days

**2** How many hours are in $4\frac{1}{2}$ days? How many seconds are in $4\frac{1}{2}$ days?

1 minute = 60 seconds
1 hour = 60 minutes
1 day = 24 hours
1 week = 7 days

# TAKING ON THE B.E.S.T.

**MA.5.M.I.1** | **Math Missions** | **Measurement Conversions**

## PART ONE

Jophiel needs at least 12.5 yards of string lights for her backyard patio. One strand of lights has a length of 100 inches. How many strands of lights will she need to order?

1 foot = 12 inches
1 yard = 3 feet
1 mile = 5,280 feet
1 mile = 1,760 yards

_____
_____
_____
_____

## PART TWO

After Jophiel receives her order. It takes her 0.25 hours to hang each strand of light. How many seconds did it take for her to hang all of the strands that she orders?

1 minute = 60 seconds
1 hour = 60 minutes
1 day = 24 hours
1 week = 7 days

_____
_____
_____
_____

# TAKING ON THE B.E.S.T.

## Math Misconception Mystery
## (PAGE 1)

**BEFORE THE VIDEO:** Solve the problem on your own.

Alice needs 30 ounces of lemon juice for her most delicious dessert. She can only measure with a yellow container that holds $\frac{1}{4}$ cup of liquid. How many times must she fill the yellow container with lemon juice to get the correct amount?

1 cup = 8 fluid ounces
1 pint = 2 cups
1 quart = 2 pints
1 gallon = 4 quarts

**DURING THE VIDEO:** Pause after each "character" solves the problem and jot down quick notes to help you remember what they did correctly or incorrectly.

Character #1 _____

Character #2 _____

Character #3 _____

Character #4 _____

# TAKING ON THE B.E.S.T.

## MA.5.M.1.1 — Math Misconception Mystery (PAGE 2)

**AFTER THE VIDEO:** Discuss and analyze their answers.

The most reasonable answer belongs to Character # _____ because

_____

_____

_____

_____

(Justify how this character's work makes sense.)

### Let's help the others:

|  | Character #___: | Character #___: | Character #___: |
|---|---|---|---|
| What did this character do that was correct? |  |  |  |
| Identify their error |  |  |  |
| What do they need to know to understand for next time? |  |  |  |

# TAKING ON THE B.E.S.T.

**MA.5.M.2.1**  **Video Lesson** **Real-World Problems with Money**

**1** Drake has 2 ten-dollar bills, 3 five-dollar bills, 4 one-dollar bills, 3 quarters, 5 dimes, 2 nickels, and 9 pennies. He wants to purchase 4 shirts that cost $9.90 each. Does he have enough?

**2** For Matt's birthday, he received a twenty-dollar bill and a $25 gift card to his favorite restaurant. He goes out to dinner at his favorite restaurant, and orders two steak dinners for $12.25 each. He includes a tip of $5.15. How much money will Matt have left after paying for his dinner?

**3** Mrs. Wertz buys a key lime pie for $9.58 and one gallon of lemonade for $2.76. If she hands the cashier a ten dollar bill and six half-dollars, how much change will she receive back?

# TAKING ON THE B.E.S.T.

| MA.5.M.2.1 | Extra Practice #1 | Real-World Problems with Money |
| --- | --- | --- |

**1** Marta has 4 ten−dollar bills, 5 five−dollar bills, 8 one−dollar bills, 8 quarters, 7 dimes, 12 nickels, and 39 pennies. She wants to purchase 5 books for a total of $80.69. Does she have enough?

**2** For Mr. Keys birthday, he received 2 twenty−dollar bills and a $50 gift card to a clothing store. Mr. Keys purchased three shirts for a total of $66.30. If each shirt cost the same amount, how much was each shirt? How much money will Mr. Keys have after he pays for his shirts?

**3** Carter buys two packs of paper towels for $4.46 each and two gallons of milk for $3.99 each. If he hands the cashier a twenty−dollar bill, what bills and coins could he receive back as change?

227

# TAKING ON THE B.E.S.T.

| MA.5.M.2.1 | Extra Practice #2 | Real-World Problems with Money |

**1** Robyn has 3 twenty–dollar bills, 5 ten–dollar bills, 3 quarters, 4 dimes, 2 nickels, and 63 pennies. She runs errands for her four neighbors and receives the same amount from each of them. Now she has exactly $187.88. How much money did she receive from each neighbors?

**2** Luke purchases four pairs of socks for $2.75 each and three chocolate bars for $0.80 each. How much money does he spend?

**3** Andrea purchases four body boards for $12.85 each and a package of beach toys for $2.60. She hands the cashier 3 twenty–dollar bills and 8 quarters. What possible bills and coins could she receive back in change?

228

# TAKING ON THE B.E.S.T.

**MA.5.M.2.1** | **Math Missions** | **Real-World Problems with Money**

Chelsea wants to purchase equipment to record videos. Below is her list of equipment costs:

- ☐ Microphone = $13.98
- ☐ Camera = $496.87
- ☐ Lighting = $159.97
- ☐ Editing software = $15.90 each month
- ☐ Tripod = $24.88
- ☐ Membership to film course = $9.75 each month

## PART ONE

If Chelsea plans to study and practice filming for one year, how much should she plan to save for the equipment, software, and film course?

_____

_____

_____

_____

_____

## PART TWO

Chelsea has $315.69 saved up in her account. How much more does she need to save in order to buy all the equipment and one month of software and membership to the film course?

_____

_____

_____

_____

# TAKING ON THE B.E.S.T.

## MA.5.M.2.1 | Math Misconception Mystery (PAGE 1)

**BEFORE THE VIDEO:** Solve the problem on your own.

> Mr. Feeny wants to buy pizza. He needs at least 20 slices. He can buy boxes of pizza with 8 slices for $10.35 a box. Slices of pizza are also available for $1.75 each. Would it be cheaper for him to buy pizza boxes or individual slices? Explain your thinking.

**DURING THE VIDEO:** Pause after each "character" solves the problem and jot down quick notes to help you remember what they did correctly or incorrectly.

| Character #1 _____ | Character #2 _____ |
|---|---|
| | |
| Character #3 _____ | Character #4 _____ |
| | |

# TAKING ON THE B.E.S.T.

**Math Misconception Mystery (PAGE 2)**

**AFTER THE VIDEO:** Discuss and analyze their answers.

The most reasonable answer belongs to Character # _____ because

_____

_____

_____

_____

(Justify how this character's work makes sense.)

## Let's help the others:

|  | Character #___: | Character #___: | Character #___: |
|---|---|---|---|
| What did this character do that was correct? |  |  |  |
| Identify their error |  |  |  |
| What do they need to know to understand for next time? |  |  |  |

231

# TAKING ON THE B.E.S.T.

Identify the correct name of each triangle based on its angles. Include a brief description of each.

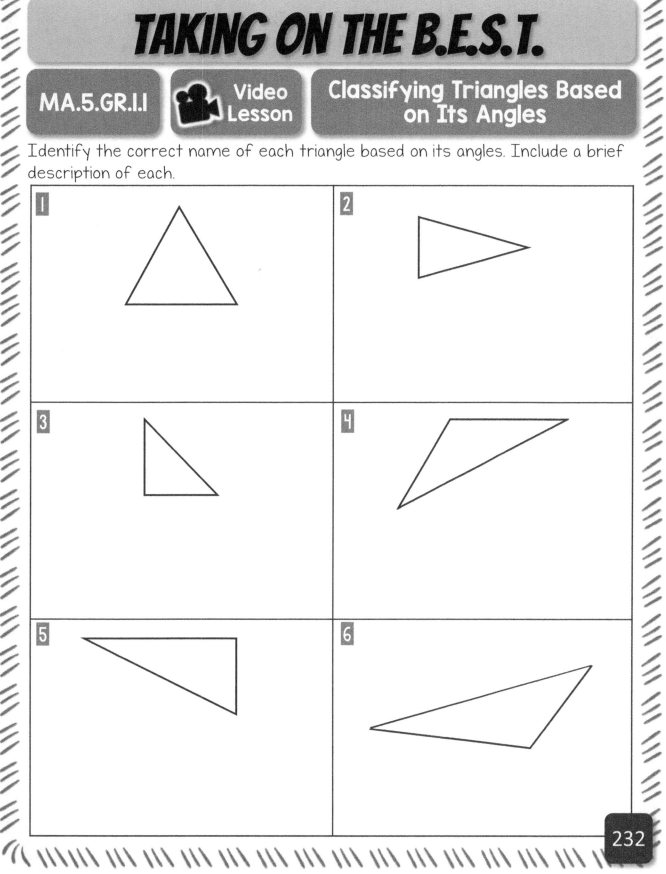

# TAKING ON THE B.E.S.T.

  Video Lesson | Classifying Triangles Based on Its Sides

Identify the correct name of each triangle based on its sides. Include a brief description of each.

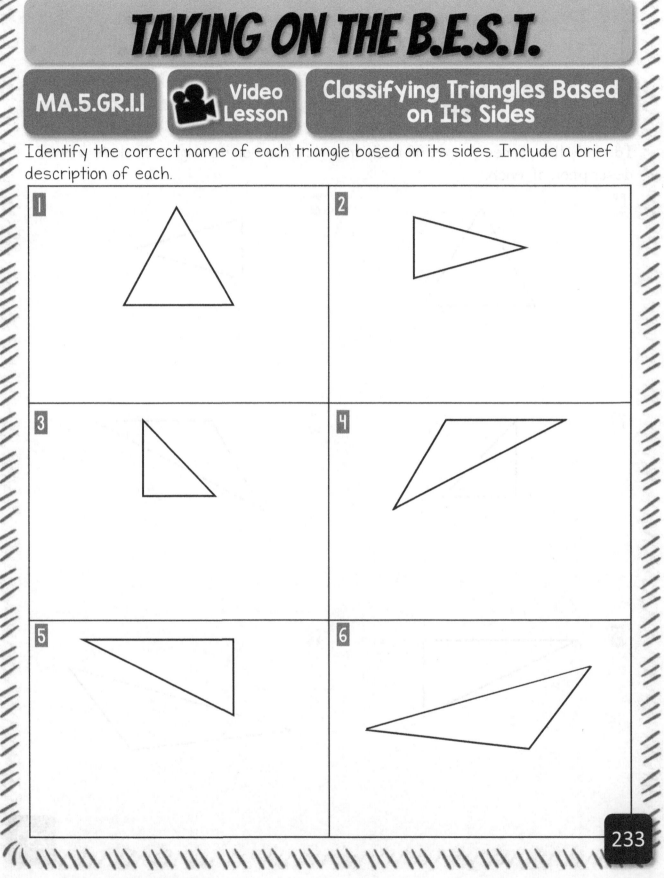

233

# TAKING ON THE B.E.S.T.

**Extra Practice #1** **Classifying Triangles Based on Angles and Sides**

Select all the names that can be used to classify each triangle.

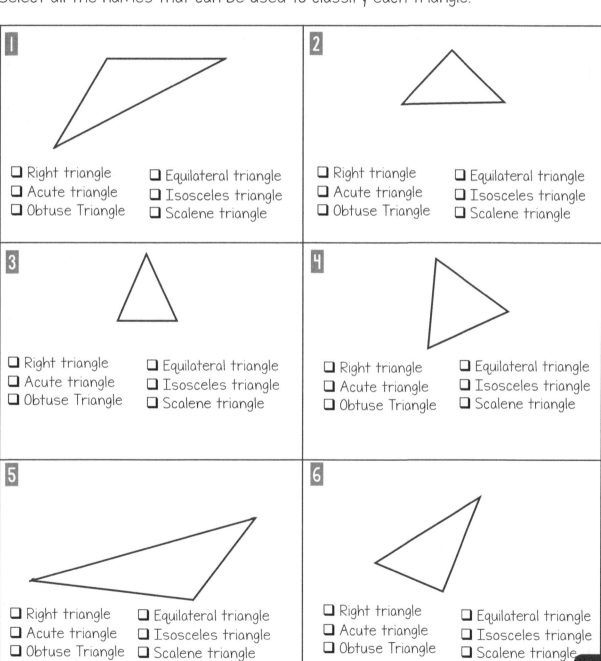

**1**

- ❏ Right triangle
- ❏ Acute triangle
- ❏ Obtuse Triangle
- ❏ Equilateral triangle
- ❏ Isosceles triangle
- ❏ Scalene triangle

**2**

- ❏ Right triangle
- ❏ Acute triangle
- ❏ Obtuse Triangle
- ❏ Equilateral triangle
- ❏ Isosceles triangle
- ❏ Scalene triangle

**3**

- ❏ Right triangle
- ❏ Acute triangle
- ❏ Obtuse Triangle
- ❏ Equilateral triangle
- ❏ Isosceles triangle
- ❏ Scalene triangle

**4**

- ❏ Right triangle
- ❏ Acute triangle
- ❏ Obtuse Triangle
- ❏ Equilateral triangle
- ❏ Isosceles triangle
- ❏ Scalene triangle

**5**

- ❏ Right triangle
- ❏ Acute triangle
- ❏ Obtuse Triangle
- ❏ Equilateral triangle
- ❏ Isosceles triangle
- ❏ Scalene triangle

**6**

- ❏ Right triangle
- ❏ Acute triangle
- ❏ Obtuse Triangle
- ❏ Equilateral triangle
- ❏ Isosceles triangle
- ❏ Scalene triangle

Use this graphic organizer to classify quadrilaterals.

# TAKING ON THE B.E.S.T.

| Extra Practice #2 | Classifying Quadrilaterals

Use the following terms to classify each figure below: polygon, quadrilateral, trapezoid, parallelogram, rectangle, rhombus, and square.

| | |
|---|---|
| 1 | 2 |
| 3 | 4 |
| 5 | 6 |

236

# TAKING ON THE B.E.S.T.

**MA.5.GR.1.1** | **Extra Practice #3** | **Classifying Quadrilaterals**

**1** Why is a square always a rhombus? Why is a rhombus not always a square?

_____

_____

_____

_____

**2** Why is a parallelogram always a trapezoid? Why is a trapezoid not always parallelogram?

_____

_____

_____

_____

**3** Why is a rectangle sometimes a square, but not always?

_____

_____

_____

_____

# TAKING ON THE B.E.S.T.

**MA.5.GR.I.I** | **Math Missions** | **Classify Triangles and Quadrilaterals**

## PART ONE

Use "sometimes, always, or never" to make each statement true. Provide additional reasoning to justify your thinking.

• An acute triangle is _____ a equilateral triangle.

_____

_____

• An isosceles triangle is _____ an obtuse triangle.

_____

_____

## PART TWO

Use "sometimes, always, or never" to make each statement true. Provide additional reasoning to justify your thinking.

• A parallelogram is _____ a rhombus.

_____

_____

• A quadrilateral is _____ polygon.

_____

_____

238

# TAKING ON THE B.E.S.T.

**Math Misconception Mystery (PAGE 1)**

**BEFORE THE VIDEO:** Solve the problem on your own.

> Which statement about a rhombus is always true?
> Ⓐ A square is always a rhombus.
> Ⓑ A parallelogram is never a rhombus.
> Ⓒ A rectangle is always a rhombus.
> Ⓓ A rhombus is sometimes a quadrilateral.

**DURING THE VIDEO:** Pause after each "character" solves the problem and jot down quick notes to help you remember what they did correctly or incorrectly.

| Character #1 _____ | Character #2 _____ |
|---|---|
| | |
| **Character #3** _____ | **Character #4** _____ |
| | |

# TAKING ON THE B.E.S.T.

## Math Misconception Mystery
### (PAGE 2)

**AFTER THE VIDEO:** Discuss and analyze their answers.

The most reasonable answer belongs to Character # _____ because

_____

_____

_____

_____

(Justify how this character's work makes sense.)

### Let's help the others:

|  | Character #___: | Character #___: | Character #___: |
|---|---|---|---|
| What did this character do that was correct? |  |  |  |
| Identify their error |  |  |  |
| What do they need to know to understand for next time? |  |  |  |

240

# TAKING ON THE B.E.S.T.

Identify the correct name of each three-dimensional figures based on their attributes (i.e. faces, bases, whether or not there is an apex, edges)

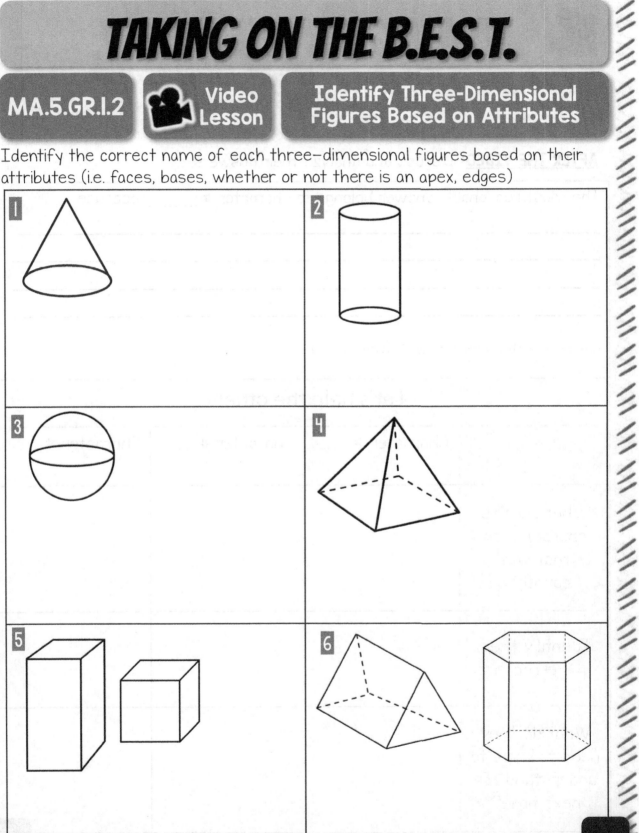

# TAKING ON THE B.E.S.T.

Name each three–dimensional figure. Provide three attributes that can describe each figure.

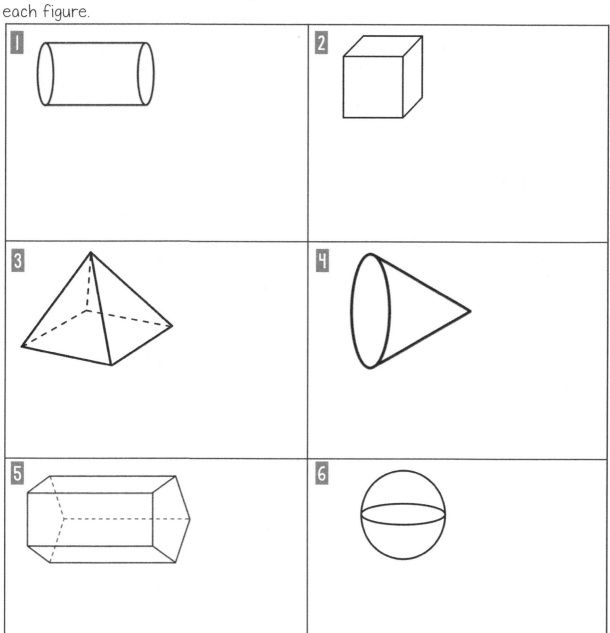

1

2

3

4

5

6

# TAKING ON THE B.E.S.T.

  **Video Lesson** | **Classify Three-Dimensional Figures Based on Attributes**

Determine whether each three–dimensional figure contains the listed attributes.

| | Contains an Apex | Contains Circular Face/ Base | Contains Rectangular Face/ Base | Contains Straight Edges | Contains No Faces | Contains a Vertex or Vertices |
|---|---|---|---|---|---|---|
| (rectangular prism) | | | | | | |
| (cylinder) | | | | | | |
| (pyramid) | | | | | | |

243

**MA.5.GR.1.2** | **Extra Practice #2** | **Classify Three-Dimensional Figures Based on Attributes**

Determine whether each three-dimensional figure contains the listed attributes.

|  | Contains an Apex | Contains Circular Face/ Base | Contains Rectangular Face/ Base | Contains Straight Edges | Contains Curved Surfaces | Contains a Vertex or Vertices |
|---|---|---|---|---|---|---|
| cone |  |  |  |  |  |  |
| triangular prism |  |  |  |  |  |  |
| hexagonal prism |  |  |  |  |  |  |

# TAKING ON THE B.E.S.T.

| MA.5.GR.I.2 | Math Missions | Classify Three-Dimensional Figures Based on Attributes |
|---|---|---|

## PART ONE

Label each three–dimensional figure below. Based on their attributes, what do they have in common? How are they different?

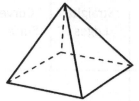 

_____

_____

_____

_____

## PART TWO

Chris says, "The three–dimensional figure below is a right prism because it contains rectangular faces with two parallel bases of the same shape. It has straight edges and an apex."

Describe Chris's error on the lines below.

_____

_____

_____

_____

# TAKING ON THE B.E.S.T.

## Math Misconception Mystery (PAGE I)

**BEFORE THE VIDEO:** Solve the problem on your own.

> Select all the shapes that contain a circular face.
> (A) Sphere
> (B) Right circular cones
> (C) Right pyramids
> (D) Right circular cylinders
> (E) Right prisms

**DURING THE VIDEO:** Pause after each "character" solves the problem and jot down quick notes to help you remember what they did correctly or incorrectly.

| Character #1 _____ | Character #2 _____ |
|---|---|
| | |
| **Character #3** _____ | **Character #4** _____ |
| | |

# TAKING ON THE B.E.S.T.

**MA.5.GR.I.2** | **Math Misconception Mystery (PAGE 2)**

**AFTER THE VIDEO:** Discuss and analyze their answers.

The most reasonable answer belongs to Character # _____ because

_____

_____

_____

_____

(Justify how this character's work makes sense.)

## Let's help the others:

| | Character #___: | Character #___: | Character #___: |
|---|---|---|---|
| What did this character do that was correct? | | | |
| Identify their error | | | |
| What do they need to know to understand for next time? | | | |

# TAKING ON THE B.E.S.T.

  **Video Lesson** **Perimeter & Area of Rectangles with Fractional Side Lengths**

**1** Martin buys a blank canvas for his new painting. The dimensions of the canvas are shown below. Find the perimeter and the area of the blank canvas.

$\frac{3}{4}$ ft

$\frac{2}{3}$ ft

**2** Find the perimeter and the area of the square window below.

$\frac{5}{6}$ yd

# TAKING ON THE B.E.S.T.

**1** Francis has a white, square tile that he is going to decorate. The length of the tile is shown below. Find the perimeter and the area.

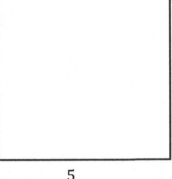

$\dfrac{5}{10}$ ft

**2** Find the perimeter and the area of the rectangular field.

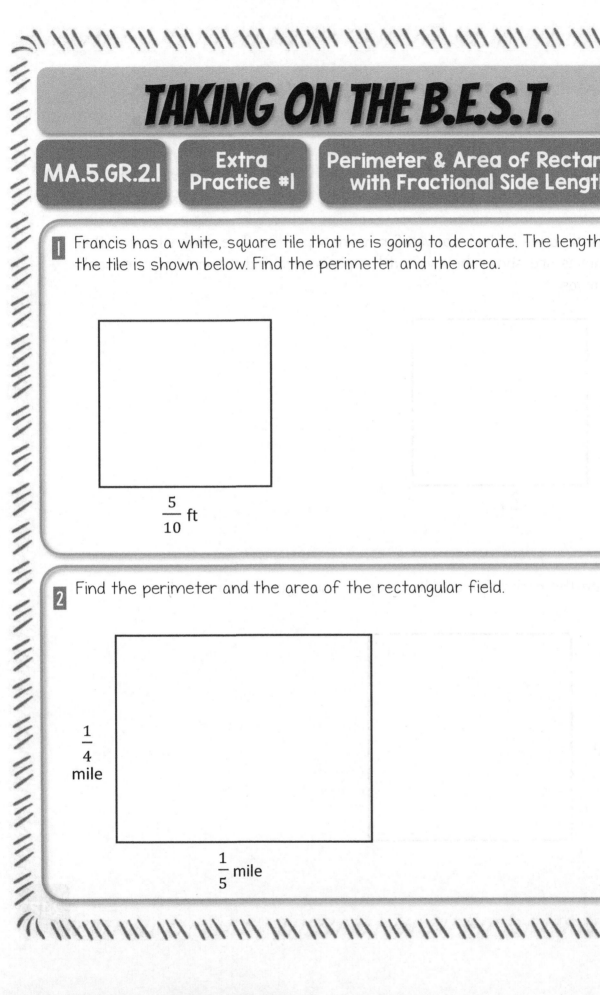

$\dfrac{1}{4}$ mile

$\dfrac{1}{5}$ mile

# TAKING ON THE B.E.S.T.

**1** Iliana purchases a new rug for her room. The dimensions of the new rug are shown below. Find the perimeter and the area of the new rug.

5.6 ft

6.7 ft

**2** Daniel builds a square dance floor with a length of 7.4 yards. Find the perimeter and the area of Daniel's dance floor.

**1** Josefina visits a mural downtown. The height of the mural is 9.4 yards. The length of the mural is 8.2 yards. What is the perimeter and area of mural?

**2** Lucy creates a square garden. One side-length of the garden is 7.3 feet. Help Lucy find the area and the perimeter of her square garden.

# TAKING ON THE B.E.S.T.

Xavier draws a rectangle in the sand at the beach. He measures the length of his rectangle and determines it is 16.4 inches. The width of his rectangle is exactly half of the length.

## PART ONE

Draw a picture of Xavier's sand rectangle and label it with the dimensions.

## PART TWO

Xavier says the perimeter of his rectangle is 24.6 inches. Is he correct or incorrect? Explain your thinking on the lines below.

_____

_____

_____

_____

## PART THREE

What is the area of Xavier's sand rectangle?

# TAKING ON THE B.E.S.T.

| MA.5.GR.2.1 | Math Misconception Mystery (PAGE 1) |
|---|---|

**BEFORE THE VIDEO:** Solve the problem on your own.

What is the perimeter and area of the square below?

0.6 m

**DURING THE VIDEO:** Pause after each "character" solves the problem and jot down quick notes to help you remember what they did correctly or incorrectly.

Character #1 _____

Character #2 _____

Character #3 _____

Character #4 _____

# TAKING ON THE B.E.S.T.

**Math Misconception Mystery (PAGE 2)**

**AFTER THE VIDEO:** Discuss and analyze their answers.

The most reasonable answer belongs to Character # _____ because

_____

_____

_____

_____

(Justify how this character's work makes sense.)

## Let's help the others:

| | Character #___: | Character #___: | Character #___: |
|---|---|---|---|
| What did this character do that was correct? | | | |
| Identify their error | | | |
| What do they need to know to understand for next time? | | | |

# TAKING ON THE B.E.S.T.

 Video Lesson

## Finding Volume by Counting Cubes

Several examples of rectangular prisms are shown below. Use the layers to determine the number of unit cubes it will take to fill the container completely without any gaps or overlaps. This will give you the volume of the rectangular prism.

**1**

one layer        two layers fill the box

**2**

one layer        three layers fill the box

**3**

one layer        four layers fill the box

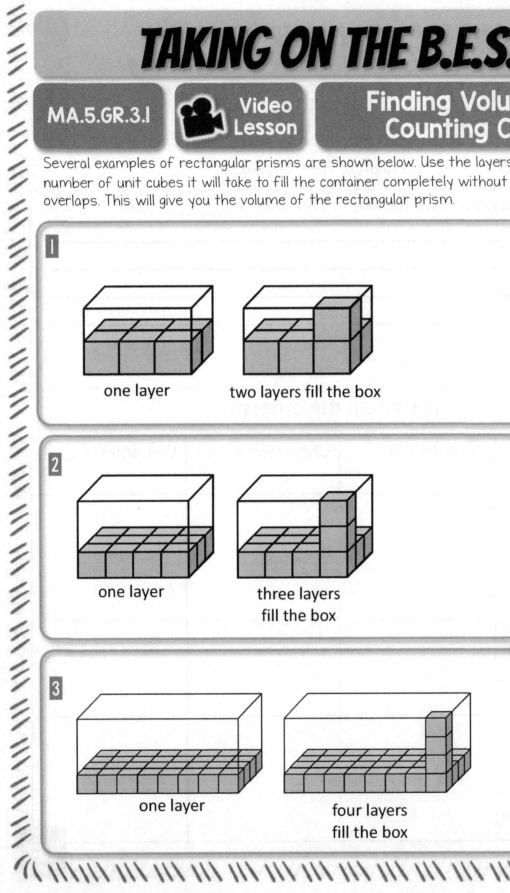

# TAKING ON THE B.E.S.T.

**Extra Practice #1** **Finding Volume by Counting Cubes**

Several examples of rectangular prisms are shown below. Use the layers to determine the number of unit cubes it will take to fill the container completely without any gaps or overlaps. This will give you the volume of the rectangular prism.

1

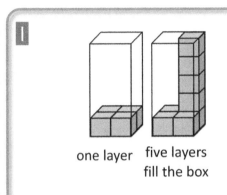

one layer    five layers fill the box

2

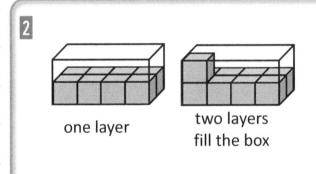

one layer    two layers fill the box

3

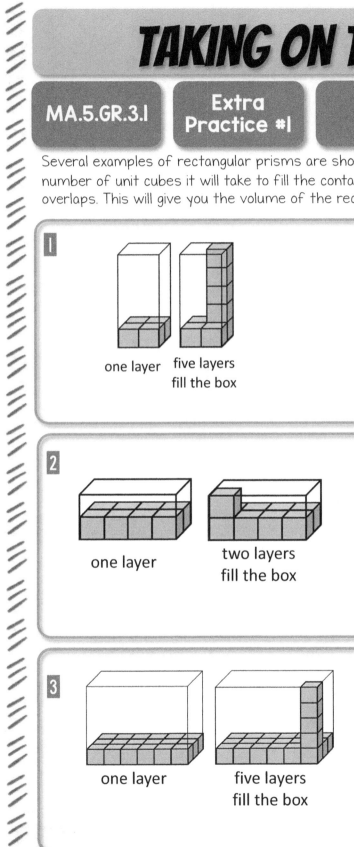

one layer    five layers fill the box

# TAKING ON THE B.E.S.T.

Several examples of rectangular prisms are shown below. Count the cubes to determine the volume of each rectangular prism.

1

2
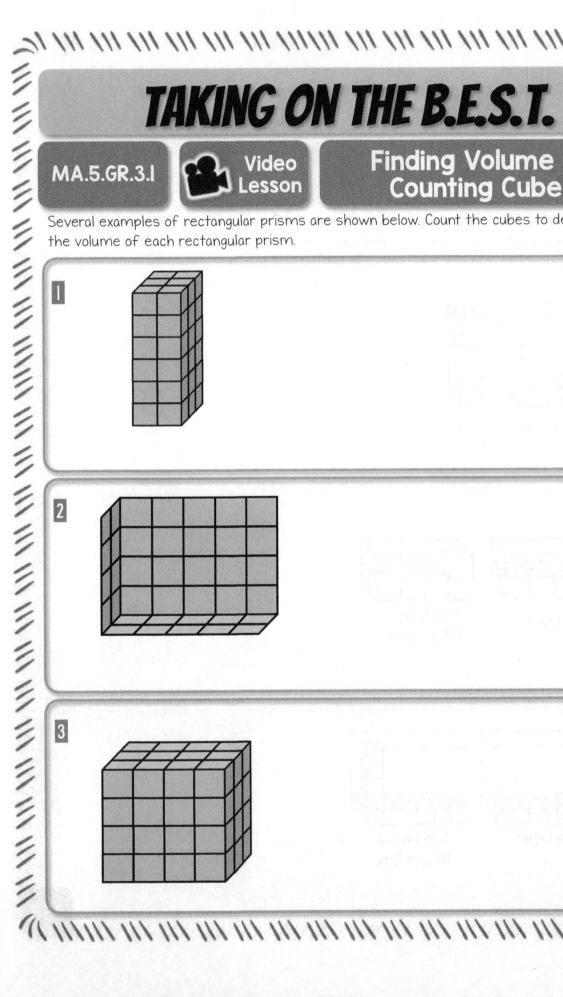

3
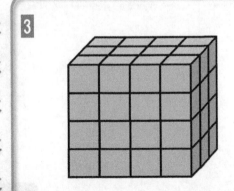

# TAKING ON THE B.E.S.T.

## Finding Volume by Counting Cubes

Several examples of rectangular prisms are shown below. Count the cubes to determine the volume of each rectangular prism.

**1**

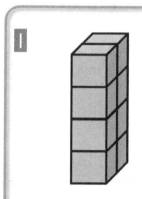

**2**

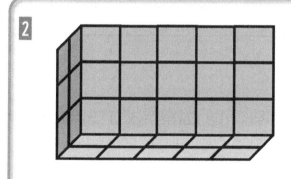

**3**

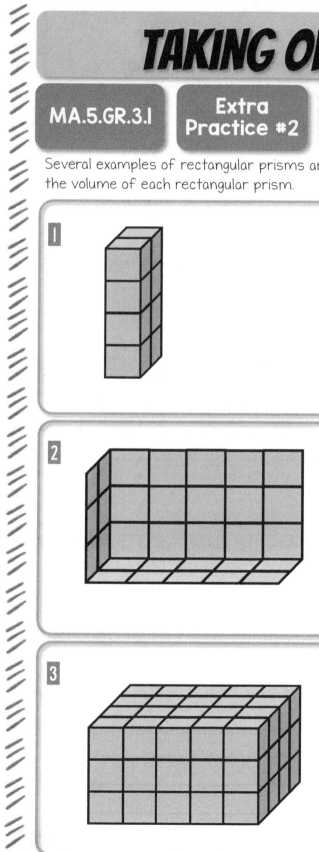

# TAKING ON THE B.E.S.T.

## PART ONE

Will has a box shaped like a rectangular prism. He packs the box with toy blocks each shaped like a cube. Each toy block has a volume of 1 cubic inch. The first layer of blocks can hold exactly 4 rows of 5 toy blocks each. Will has 150 toy blocks. If the box can hold 7 layers of blocks, can Will fit all of his toy blocks in the large box? Explain your thinking.

_____

_____

_____

_____

## PART TWO

August has 135 toy blocks to pack. If he is using the same-sized box as Will, how many more toy blocks can the box hold once August has packed all of his toy blocks? Explain your thinking.

_____

_____

_____

_____

259

# TAKING ON THE B.E.S.T.

## Math Misconception Mystery
### (PAGE 1)

**BEFORE THE VIDEO:** Solve the problem on your own.

What is the volume of the right rectangular prism?

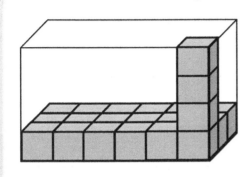

**DURING THE VIDEO:** Pause after each "character" solves the problem and jot down quick notes to help you remember what they did correctly or incorrectly.

Character #1 _____

Character #2 _____

Character #3 _____

Character #4 _____

# TAKING ON THE B.E.S.T.

| MA.5.GR.3.1 | Math Misconception Mystery (PAGE 2) |

**AFTER THE VIDEO:** Discuss and analyze their answers.

The most reasonable answer belongs to Character # _____ because

_____

_____

_____

_____

(Justify how this character's work makes sense.)

## Let's help the others:

|  | Character #___: | Character #___: | Character #___: |
|---|---|---|---|
| What did this character do that was correct? |  |  |  |
| Identify their error |  |  |  |
| What do they need to know to understand for next time? |  |  |  |

# TAKING ON THE B.E.S.T.

  **Video Lesson** | **Finding Volume Using Formulas (with Visuals)**

Several examples of rectangular prisms are shown below. Use two different formulas to determine the volume of each rectangular prism: $V = L \times W \times H$ and $V = B \times H$

**1**

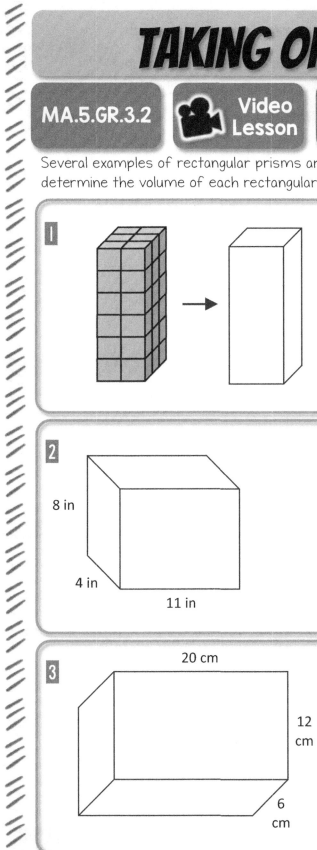

**2**

8 in

4 in

11 in

**3**

20 cm

12 cm

6 cm

| MA.5.GR.3.2 | Extra Practice #1 | Finding Volume Using Formulas (with Visuals) |

Several examples of rectangular prisms are shown below. Use two different formulas to determine the volume of each rectangular prism: $V = L \times W \times H$ and $V = B \times H$

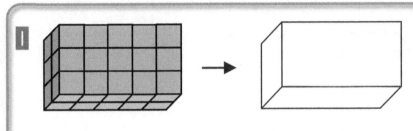

**1**

**2**

12 in

5 in

13 in

**3**

21 cm

14 cm

9 cm

**1** Vysean is holding a box with a length of 30 centimeters, a height of 15 centimeters, and a width of 13 centimeters. What is the volume of Vysean's box?

**2** Darlene's fish tank is 3 feet tall, 3 feet wide, and 8 feet long. What is the volume of Darlene's tank?

**3** Mrs. McCallister rents a storage room that is 12 feet wide and 11 feet long. The storage room is 9 feet high. What is the volume of Mrs. McCallister's storage room?

**1** Paul's bathroom cabinet is 18 inches long and 4 inches wide. The height is 15 inches tall. What is the volume of Paul's bathroom cabinet?

**2** Walter has a foldable storage shelf that has a base of 80 square inches. The foldable storage shelf is 11 inches tall. Find the volume of Walter's foldable storage shelf.

**3** Ian receives a package in the mail in the shape of a rectangular prism. The package has dimensions with a height of 9 centimeters, a width of 16 centimeters, and a length of 25 centimeters. What is the volume of Ian's package?

# TAKING ON THE B.E.S.T.

**MA.5.GR.3.2** | **Math Missions** | **Finding Volume Using Formulas**

Use the cards below to create a three 2-digit numbers to represent the unit dimensions of a rectangular prism.

## CARDS

2 3 4 5 6 7

## PART ONE

Using the cards provided, what is the smallest volume you can create, in cubic units? Explain your reasoning.

_____

_____

_____

_____

## PART TWO

Using the cards provided, what is the greatest volume you can create, in cubic units? Explain your reasoning.

_____

_____

_____

_____

# TAKING ON THE B.E.S.T.

**BEFORE THE VIDEO:** Solve the problem on your own.

What is the volume of the right rectangular prism?

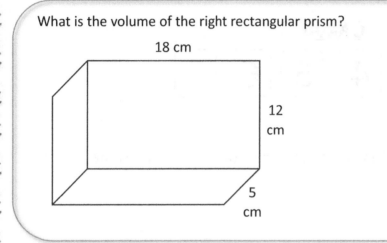

18 cm

12 cm

5 cm

**DURING THE VIDEO:** Pause after each "character" solves the problem and jot down quick notes to help you remember what they did correctly or incorrectly.

| Character #1 _____ | Character #2 _____ |
|---|---|
| | |
| **Character #3** _____ | **Character #4** _____ |
| | |

# TAKING ON THE B.E.S.T.

## MA.5.GR.3.2 | Math Misconception Mystery (PAGE 2)

**AFTER THE VIDEO:** Discuss and analyze their answers.

The most reasonable answer belongs to Character # _____ because

_____

_____

_____

_____

(Justify how this character's work makes sense.)

### Let's help the others:

|  | Character #___: | Character #___: | Character #___: |
|---|---|---|---|
| What did this character do that was correct? |  |  |  |
| Identify their error |  |  |  |
| What do they need to know to understand for next time? |  |  |  |

# TAKING ON THE B.E.S.T.

MA.5.GR.3.3  Video Lesson | Real-World Volume Problems with an Unknown Edge Length

Gemma places three grocery items on the counter that she picked up from the store. They are all in the shape of a rectangular prism. Use the volume and given dimensions to find the unknown length. Write an equation using a variable and solve.

**1**

Volume = 392 cubic centimeters

Milk

14 cm

7 cm

**2**

Volume = 288 cubic centimeters

Cream Cheese

4 cm

12 cm

**3**

Volume = 560 cubic centimeters

Cereal

Base 112 square cm

# TAKING ON THE B.E.S.T.

**MA.5.GR.3.3** | **Extra Practice #1** | **Real-World Volume Problems with an Unknown Edge Length**

Gemma places three grocery items on the counter that she picked up from the store. They are all in the shape of a rectangular prism. Use the volume and given dimensions to find the unknown length. Write an equation using a variable and solve.

**1**                                     Volume = 468 cubic centimeters

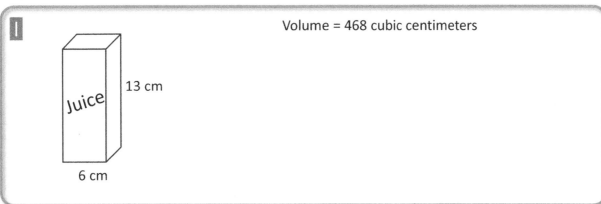

13 cm
Juice
6 cm

**2**                                     Volume = 280 cubic centimeters

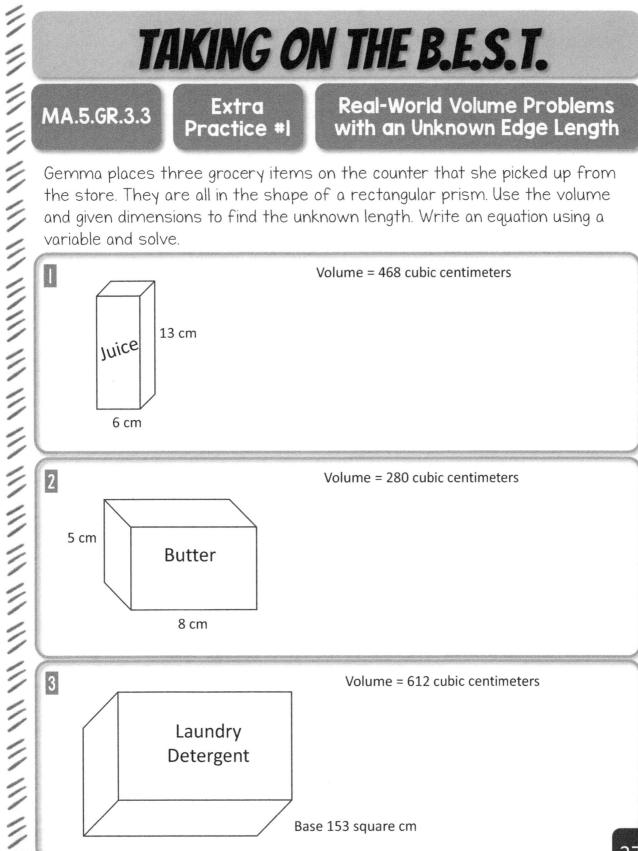

5 cm
Butter
8 cm

**3**                                     Volume = 612 cubic centimeters

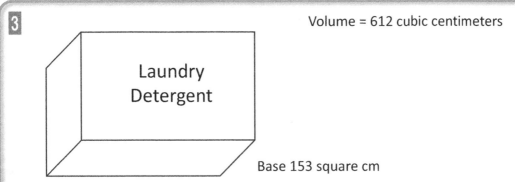

Laundry
Detergent

Base 153 square cm

270

# TAKING ON THE B.E.S.T.

**1** Jacob's tank for his iguana is 5 feet deep and 4 feet wide. The volume of his tank is 240 cubic feet. What is the length of the tank for his iguana?

**2** Pepper is holding a box with a length of 8 inches and a height of 16 inches. If the volume of the box is 512 cubic inches, what is the width?

**3** Mr. Otter has a storage room that has an area of 64 square feet. The volume of Mr. Otter's room is 448 cubic feet. Find the height of the storage room.

# TAKING ON THE B.E.S.T.

**1** Jacob's tank for his iguana is 7 feet deep and 3 feet wide. The volume of his tank is 231 cubic feet. What is the length of the tank for his iguana?

**2** Pepper is holding a box with a length of 7 inches and a height of 17 inches. If the volume of the box is 833 cubic inches, what is the width?

**3** Mr. Otter has a storage container that has an area of 48 square inches. The volume of Mr. Otter's room is 240 cubic inches. Find the height of the storage container.

**MA.5.GR.3.3** |  **Video Lesson** | **Find the Volume of Composite Figures (Basic)**

A pool company has two different layouts, as shown below. Which pool layout has a greater volume?

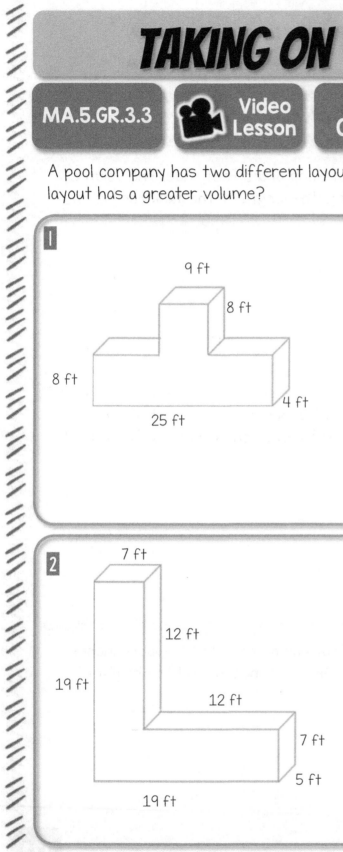

1

9 ft

8 ft

8 ft

25 ft

4 ft

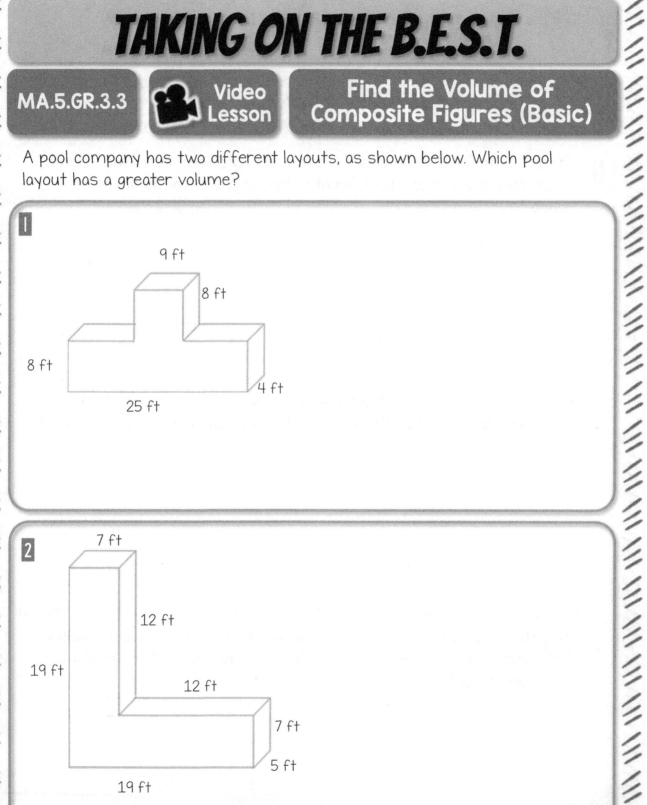

2

7 ft

12 ft

19 ft

12 ft

7 ft

5 ft

19 ft

A pool company has two different layouts, as shown below. Which pool layout has a greater volume?

**1**

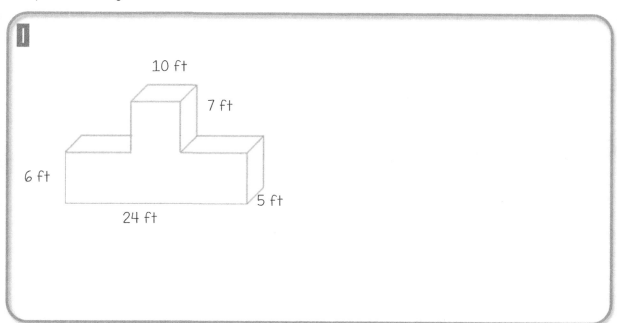

**2**

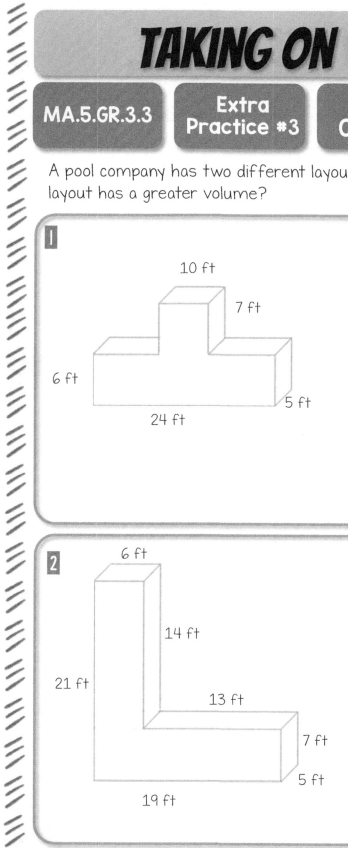

# TAKING ON THE B.E.S.T.

A pool company has two different layouts, as shown below. Which pool layout has a greater volume?

**1**

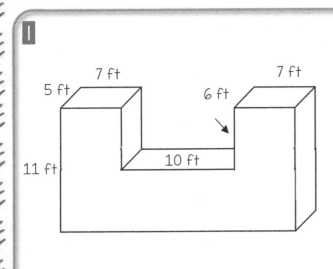

5 ft    7 ft    6 ft    7 ft

11 ft    10 ft

**2**

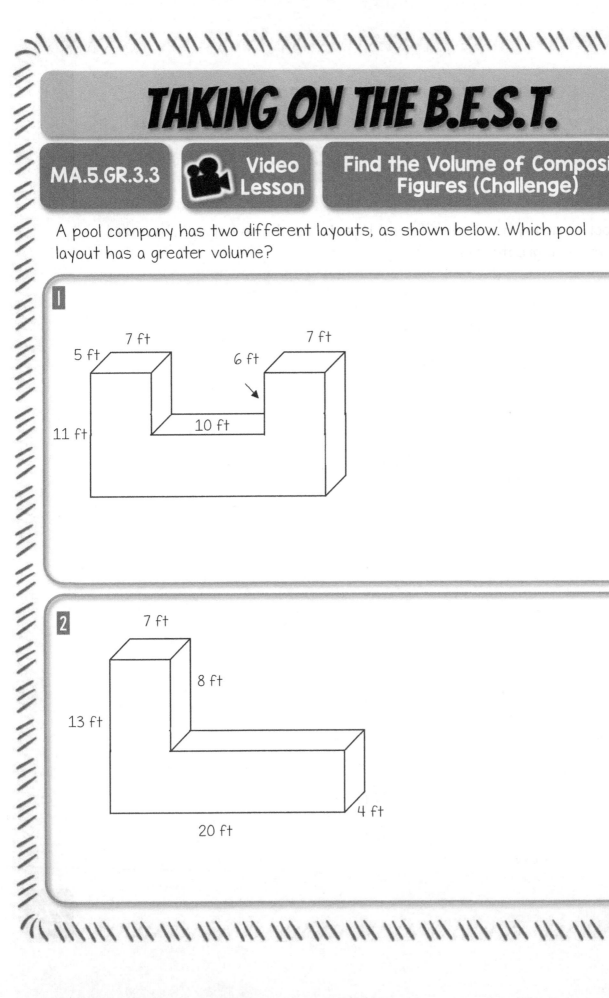

7 ft

8 ft

13 ft

20 ft

4 ft

A pool company has two different layouts, as shown below. Which pool layout has a greater volume?

**1**

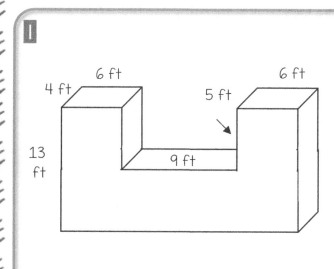

**2**

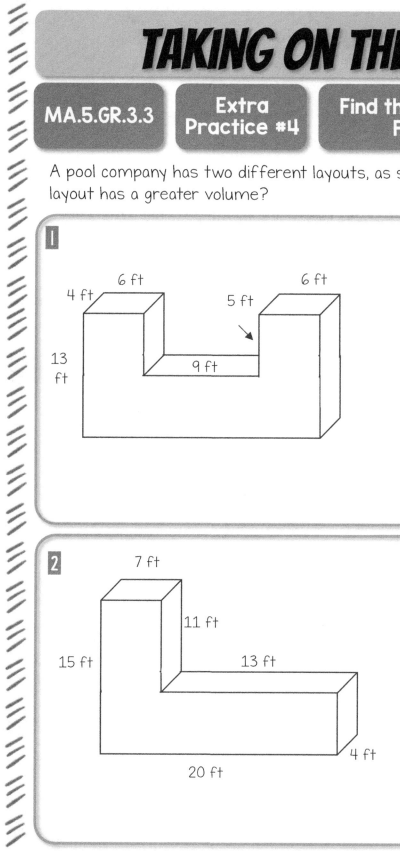

# TAKING ON THE B.E.S.T.

| MA.5.GR.3.3 | Math Missions | Volume in the Real World |
|---|---|---|

## PART ONE

Alex's bedroom has an area of 90 square feet. If the volume of his room is 720 cubic feet, what is the height of his room? Label the possible dimensions of his room on the figure below. Include an equation to determine the height, H, of his room. Then solve.

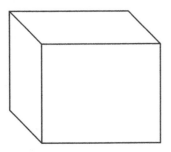

## PART TWO

Alex's parents are planning to add a closet for Alex. The plans for the closet addition are shown below. Using the dimensions you created in part one, determine the combined volume of Alex's bedroom and new closet design.

3 ft

3 ft

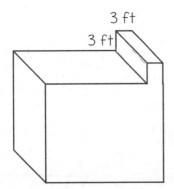

# TAKING ON THE B.E.S.T.

## Math Misconception Mystery
## (PAGE 1)

**BEFORE THE VIDEO:** Solve the problem on your own.

> The volume of a large packing box is 120 cubic feet. If the length is 6 feet an the width is 4 feet, what is the depth of the box?

**DURING THE VIDEO:** Pause after each "character" solves the problem and jot down quick notes to help you remember what they did correctly or incorrectly.

Character #1 _____

Character #2 _____

Character #3 _____

Character #4 _____

# TAKING ON THE B.E.S.T.

## Math Misconception Mystery
### (PAGE 2)

**AFTER THE VIDEO:** Discuss and analyze their answers.

The most reasonable answer belongs to Character # _____ because

_____

_____

_____

_____

(Justify how this character's work makes sense.)

## Let's help the others:

|  | Character #___: | Character #___: | Character #___: |
|---|---|---|---|
| What did this character do that was correct? |  |  |  |
| Identify their error |  |  |  |
| What do they need to know to understand for next time? |  |  |  |

279

Label the origin, x-axis, y-axis, and scale the axes with whole numbers. Finally, plot a coordinate and label it correctly.

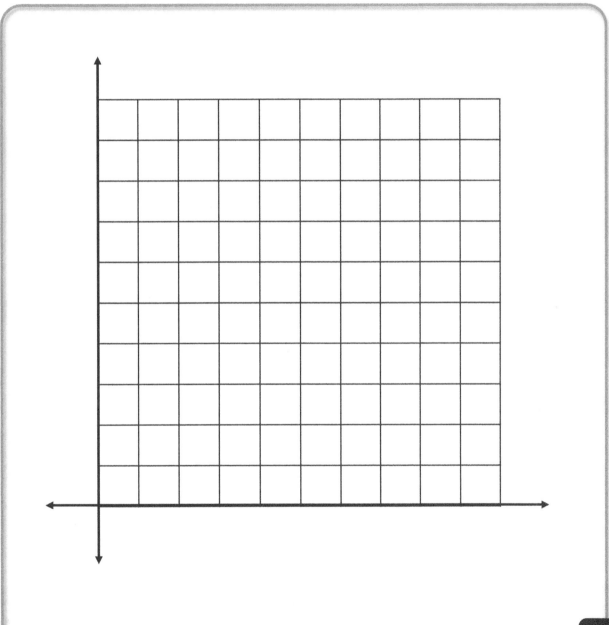

# TAKING ON THE B.E.S.T.

Extra Practice #1

## Intro to the Coordinate Plane

Label the origin, x–axis, y–axis, and scale the axes with whole numbers. Finally, plot the point (6,5) and label it correctly.

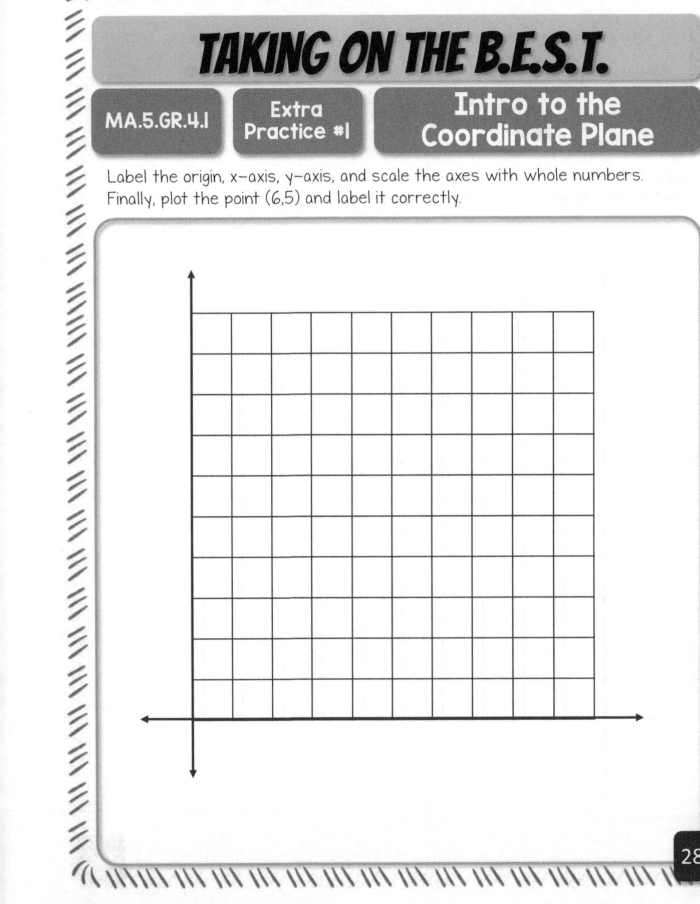

# TAKING ON THE B.E.S.T.

**MA.5.GR.4.1** | Video Lesson | **Coordinate Plane Practice**

For each practice problem, plot and label the ordered pairs correctly on the coordinate plane. Then, describe how you traveled from the origin to plot each point.

1 (1, 3)

2 (3, 1)

3 (5, 4)

# TAKING ON THE B.E.S.T.

| MA.5.GR.4.1 | Extra Practice #2 | Coordinate Plane Practice |

For each practice problem, plot and label the ordered pairs correctly on the coordinate plane. Then, describe how you traveled from the origin to plot each point.

**1** (4, 3)

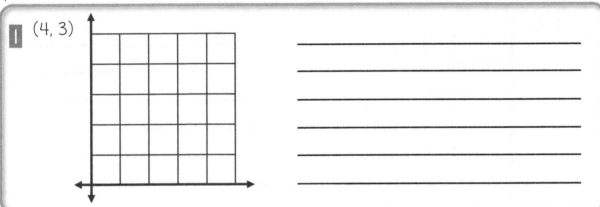

**2** (0, 2)

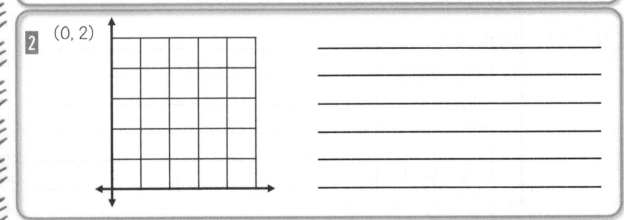

**3** (2, 5)

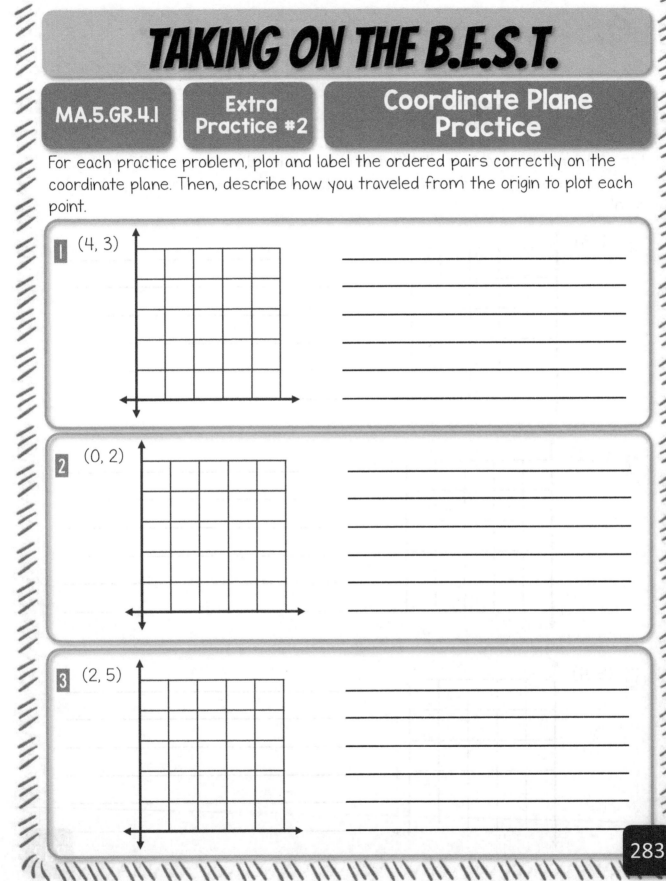

# TAKING ON THE B.E.S.T.

  **Video Lesson** **Coordinate Plane Practice with Two-Column Tables**

Label the origin, x–axis, y–axis, and scale the axes with whole numbers. Then, create coordinates using the two–column table. Finally, plot and label each coordinate.

| X | Y | COORDINATE |
|---|---|---|
| 4 | 0 | |
| 5 | 3 | |
| 6 | 1 | |
| 0 | 8 | |
| 9 | 4 | |

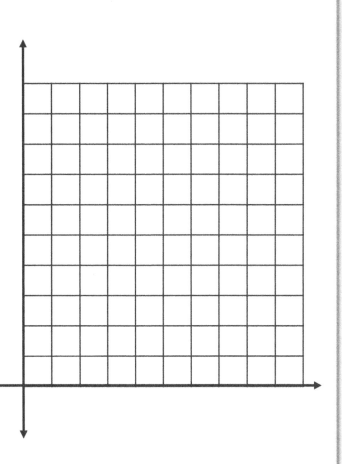

284

| MA.5.GR.4.1 | Extra Practice #3 | Coordinate Plane Practice with Two-Column Tables |

Label the origin, x–axis, y–axis, and scale the axes with whole numbers. Then, create coordinates using the two–column table. Finally, plot and label each coordinate.

| X | Y | COORDINATE |
|---|---|---|
| 3 | 3 | |
| 6 | 4 | |
| 7 | 2 | |
| 0 | 1 | |
| 6 | 0 | |

# TAKING ON THE B.E.S.T.

**MA.5.GR.4.1** | **Math Missions** | **Coordinate Plane**

## PART ONE

Plot and label the coordinate (4, 6) on the coordinate plane.

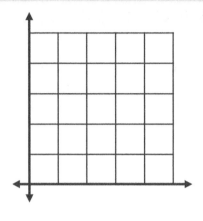

## PART TWO

Which value is the x–coordinate? What does it tell you to do?

_____

_____

Which value is the y–coordinate? What does it tell you to do?

_____

_____

## PART THREE

Lois plots the coordinate on the plane. She says, "The coordinate I plotted is (2,0)." Describe Lois's error.

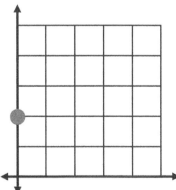

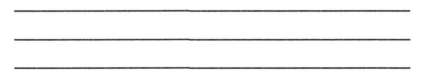

# TAKING ON THE B.E.S.T.

## MA.5.GR.4.1 | Math Misconception Mystery (PAGE 1)

**BEFORE THE VIDEO:** Solve the problem on your own.

A point has the coordinates (2, 5). If you were to plot this point, what does the 5 tell you to do?

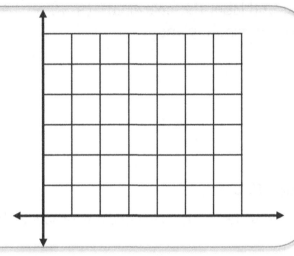

**DURING THE VIDEO:** Pause after each "character" solves the problem and jot down quick notes to help you remember what they did correctly or incorrectly.

Character #1 _____

Character #2 _____

Character #3 _____

Character #4 _____

287

# TAKING ON THE B.E.S.T.

## Math Misconception Mystery
## (PAGE 2)

**AFTER THE VIDEO:** Discuss and analyze their answers.

The most reasonable answer belongs to Character # _____ because

_____

_____

_____

_____

(Justify how this character's work makes sense.)

### Let's help the others:

|  | Character #___: | Character #___: | Character #___: |
|---|---|---|---|
| What did this character do that was correct? |  |  |  |
| Identify their error |  |  |  |
| What do they need to know to understand for next time? |  |  |  |

# TAKING ON THE B.E.S.T.

  Video Lesson | Coordinate Plane Of a Town

The map below shows the location of several places in a town.

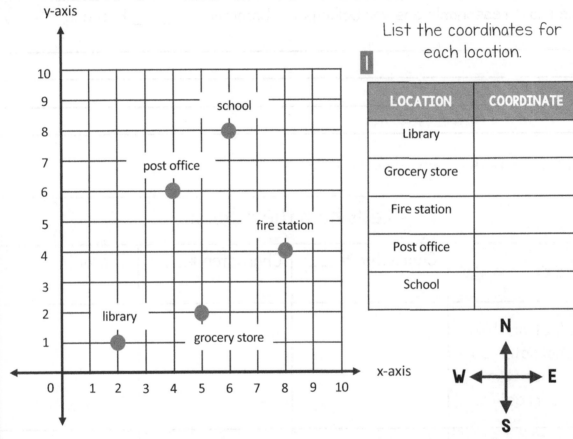

List the coordinates for each location.

| LOCATION | COORDINATE |
|---|---|
| Library | |
| Grocery store | |
| Fire station | |
| Post office | |
| School | |

1 The town is building a playground two blocks north and three blocks east from the library. What are the coordinates for the future playground?

2 The mayor wants a gas station at (0, 7). Plot and label this coordinate on the coordinate plane above.

# TAKING ON THE B.E.S.T.

| **Extra Practice #1** | **Coordinate Plane Of a Town**

The map below shows the location of several places in a town.

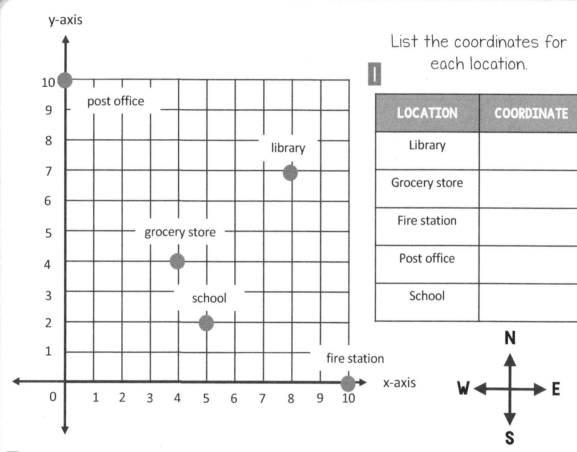

List the coordinates for each location.

**1**

| LOCATION | COORDINATE |
|---|---|
| Library | |
| Grocery store | |
| Fire station | |
| Post office | |
| School | |

**1** The town is building a hospital one block south and eight blocks west from the library. What are the coordinates for the future hospital?

**2** The mayor wants a museum at (1, 4). Plot and label this coordinate on the coordinate plane above.

# TAKING ON THE B.E.S.T.

MA.5.GR.4.2 |  Video Lesson | **Complete the Rectangle on the Coordinate Plane**

Lilly is plotting rectangles on the coordinate planes below. For each one, determine which ordered pair would represent the fourth vertex?

**1**

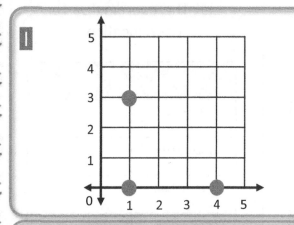

**2**

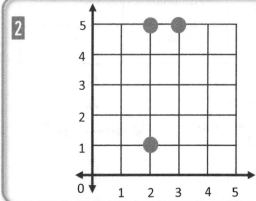

**3**

# TAKING ON THE B.E.S.T.

**MA.5.GR.4.2** | **Extra Practice #2** | **Complete the Rectangle on the Coordinate Plane**

Carly is plotting rectangles on the coordinate planes below. For each one, determine which ordered pair would represent the fourth vertex?

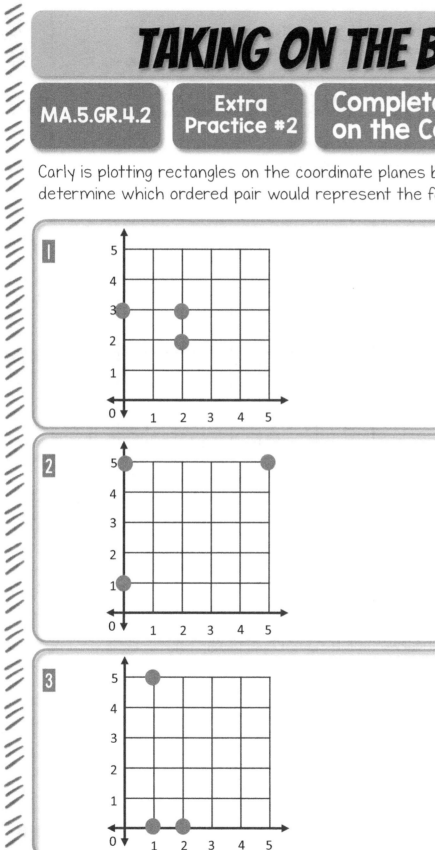

# TAKING ON THE B.E.S.T.

  **Video Lesson** **Using Coordinate Planes to Plot Data**

Marty completes two pushups every hour for 5 hours.

| HOURS | PUSHUPS |
|-------|---------|
| 1 | 2 |
| 2 | 4 |
| 3 | |
| 4 | |
| 5 | |

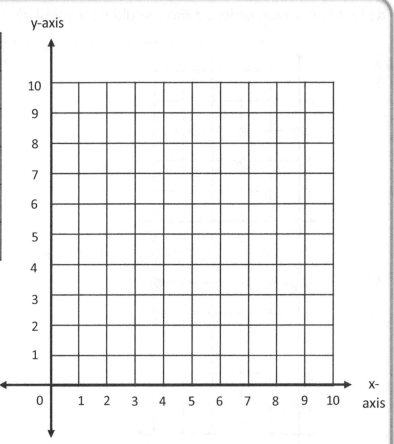

1. Help Marty complete the two-column chart.

2. Use the information in the two-column chart to create coordinates. Plot and label all five coordinates by allowing the "hours" to be represented on the x-axis and the "pushups" to be represented on the y-axis.

# TAKING ON THE B.E.S.T.

**MA.5.GR.4.2** | **Extra Practice #3** | **Using Coordinate Planes to Plot Data**

Amiko creates three bracelets every day.

| DAY | BRACELETS |
|-----|-----------|
| 1 | |
| 2 | |
| 3 | |
| 4 | |
| 5 | |

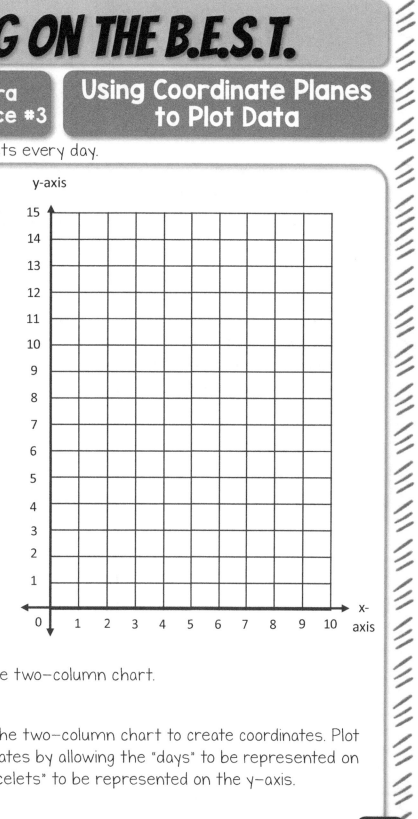

**1** Help Amiko complete the two-column chart.

**2** Use the information in the two-column chart to create coordinates. Plot and label all five coordinates by allowing the "days" to be represented on the x-axis and the "bracelets" to be represented on the y-axis.

**MA.5.GR.4.2** | **Math Missions** | **Coordinate Plane in the Real World**

Piper tracks her water consumption over the span of six hours. She drinks 2 cups of water every hour.

Make a two-column table where the first column indicates the number of hours Piper tracks her water, and the second column shows how many cups she drinks in the number of hours.

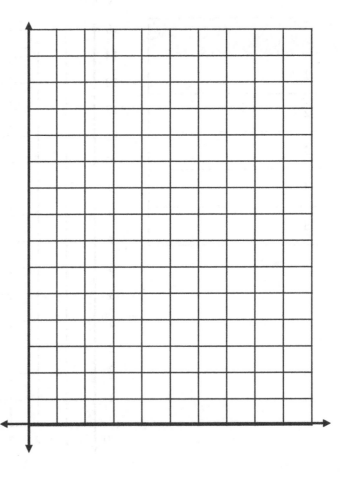

Label the coordinate plane. Then, plot points on the coordinate plane to represent your table. Decide what you want the x- and y-axis to represent.

# TAKING ON THE B.E.S.T.

## MA.5.GR.4.2 | Math Misconception Mystery (PAGE 1)

**BEFORE THE VIDEO:** Solve the problem on your own.

Mr. Barnacle is plotting a rectangle on the coordinate plane shown.

What ordered pair would represent the fourth vertex?

Ⓐ (4,5)
Ⓑ (5,4)
Ⓒ (1,1)
Ⓓ (1,4)

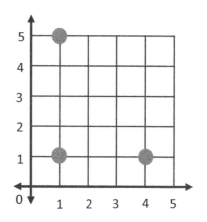

**DURING THE VIDEO:** Pause after each "character" solves the problem and jot down quick notes to help you remember what they did correctly or incorrectly.

Character #1 _____

Character #2 _____

Character #3 _____

Character #4 _____

# TAKING ON THE B.E.S.T.

| **Math Misconception Mystery (PAGE 2)**

**AFTER THE VIDEO:** Discuss and analyze their answers.

The most reasonable answer belongs to Character # _____ because

_____

_____

_____

_____

(Justify how this character's work makes sense.)

## Let's help the others:

| | Character #___: | Character #___: | Character #___: |
|---|---|---|---|
| What did this character do that was correct? | | | |
| Identify their error | | | |
| What do they need to know to understand for next time? | | | |

# TAKING ON THE B.E.S.T.

  **Video Lesson** | **Collect and Represent Data: Tables and Line Plots**

Matthew measures the lengths of 14 boards of wood, which he measured to the nearest quarter inch. He tracks his data in the table below. Represent Matthew's data in the line plot. Then, answer a few questions about the data.

| Lengths of Wooden Boards (inch) | |
|---|---|
| 12 | 11 |
| $10\frac{1}{4}$ | 12 |
| $11\frac{2}{4}$ | $10\frac{2}{4}$ |
| $10\frac{3}{4}$ | $11\frac{2}{4}$ |
| $11\frac{3}{4}$ | $11\frac{3}{4}$ |
| $11\frac{2}{4}$ | $11\frac{1}{4}$ |
| $10\frac{2}{4}$ | $11\frac{3}{4}$ |

**LINE PLOTS**

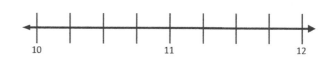

1  Describe what each X of your line plots represents.

2  What is the sum of the two second-greatest wooden boards?

Benjamin measures the lengths of 14 pencils to the nearest half centimeter. He tracks his data in the table below. Represent Benjamin's data in the line plot. Then, answer a few questions about the data.

| Lengths of Pencils (in centimeters) | |
|---|---|
| 15 | $17\frac{1}{2}$ |
| $16\frac{1}{2}$ | 18 |
| 17 | $17\frac{1}{2}$ |
| $15\frac{1}{2}$ | 15 |
| 15 | $14\frac{1}{2}$ |
| 16 | $15\frac{1}{2}$ |
| $17\frac{1}{2}$ | 15 |

**LINE PLOTS**

14    15    16    17    18

1  Describe what each X of your line plots represents.



2  What is the difference of the longest pencil and the shortest pencil?

# TAKING ON THE B.E.S.T.

Kelly records the rainfall each day over the course of five days in the table below. Represent Kelly's data in the line graph. Then, answer a few questions about the data.

| Rainfall (inches) | |
| --- | --- |
| Day 1 | 2.24 in |
| Day 2 | 2.83 in |
| Day 3 | 3.97 in |
| Day 4 | 4.49 in |
| Day 5 | 3.30 in |

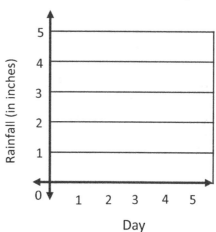

**1** What is the change in rainfall, in inches, from Day 1 to Day 2?

**2** What is the change in rainfall, in inches, from Day 4 to Day 5?

# TAKING ON THE B.E.S.T.

| MA.5.DP.I.I | Extra Practice #2 | Collect and Represent Data: Tables and Line Graphs |

Emily tracks the money she earns each day for six days. Represent Emily's data in the line graph. Then, answer a few questions about the data.

| Emily's Earnings | |
|---|---|
| Day 1 | $120. 87 |
| Day 2 | $74.12 |
| Day 3 | $23.34 |
| Day 4 | $56.18 |
| Day 5 | $67.29 |
| Day 6 | $95.06 |

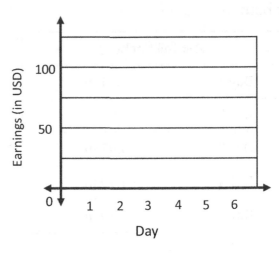

1 How much more money did Emily earn on her highest earning day compared to her lowest earning day?

2 Between which two days was there the greatest change in earnings?

# TAKING ON THE B.E.S.T.

Navaeh commits to a pushup challenge. The challenge is to complete as many pushups as possible, in 60 seconds, over the next week. Navaeh tracks her results in the table below.

Decide whether a line graph or line plot would be more appropriate to display this data, then create it.

| #PushupChallenge60 | |
|---|---|
| Monday | 9 |
| Tuesday | 6 |
| Wednesday | 6 |
| Thursday | 12 |
| Friday | 14 |
| Saturday | 16 |
| Sunday | 21 |

1. Between which two days do Navaeh's results decrease? What are your thoughts as to why this may have happened?

2. How many more pushups is Navaeh able to complete between the beginning and end of the challenge in 60 seconds?

# TAKING ON THE B.E.S.T.

## MA.5.DP.I.I | Math Misconception Mystery (PAGE I)

**BEFORE THE VIDEO:** Solve the problem on your own.

A bicycle company tracks how many bicycles they sold each month, as shown on the table below. Represent their data on the line graph.

| Bicycles Sold | |
|---|---|
| January | 56 |
| February | 99 |
| March | 12 |
| April | 30 |
| May | 55 |

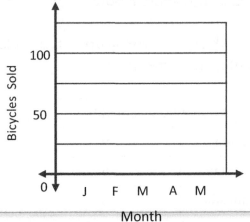

**DURING THE VIDEO:** Pause after each "character" solves the problem and jot down quick notes to help you remember what they did correctly or incorrectly.

Character #1 _____

Character #2 _____

Character #3 _____

Character #4 _____

# TAKING ON THE B.E.S.T.

| MA.5.DP.I.I | Math Misconception Mystery (PAGE 2) |

**AFTER THE VIDEO:** Discuss and analyze their answers.

The most reasonable answer belongs to Character # _____ because

_____

_____

_____

_____

(Justify how this character's work makes sense.)

## Let's help the others:

|  | Character #___: | Character #___: | Character #___: |
|---|---|---|---|
| What did this character do that was correct? |  |  |  |
| Identify their error |  |  |  |
| What do they need to know to understand for next time? |  |  |  |

| MA.5.DP.I.2 |  Video Lesson | Mode, Range, Median and Mean (Table) |

Laura tracks her scores on all of her math tests this year. The data she collects is shown below. Determine the mode, median, range and mean of Laura's data.

| Laura's Math Tests Scores | |
|---|---|
| 85 | 85 |
| 76 | 80 |
| 75 | 92 |
| 92 | 94 |
| 94 | 100 |
| 93 | 92 |

What is the mode of this set of data?

What is the median of this set of data?

What is the range of this set of data?

What is the mean of this set of data?

Isabel tracks her scores on all of her science tests this year. The data she collected is shown below. Determine the mode, median, range, and mean of Isabel's data.

| Isabel's Tests Scores | |
|---|---|
| 87 | 100 |
| 75 | 100 |
| 73 | 83 |
| 86 | 94 |
| 86 | 87 |
| 92 | 85 |

What is the mode of this set of data?

What is the median of this set of data?

What is the range of this set of data?

What is the mean of this set of data?

# TAKING ON THE B.E.S.T.

  Video Lesson | **Mean, Mode, Range, and Median (Line Plot)**

The fifth graders in Mrs. Garcia's class collected data for the amount of time they sleep on average each night. The data they collected is shown below. Determine the mode, median, range, and mean of this data.

**Time Students Sleep Nightly (in hours)**

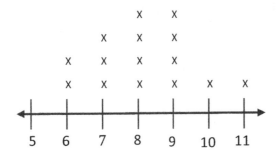

What is the mode of this set of data?

What is the median of this set of data?

What is the range of this set of data?

What is the mean of this set of data?

The fifth graders in Mrs. Reyes's class tracked the number of miles each student walked this week on the track. Determine the mode, median, and range of this data

**Distance Walked (in miles)**

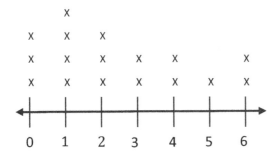

What is the mode of this set of data?

What is the median of this set of data?

What is the range of this set of data?

What is the mean of this set of data?

# TAKING ON THE B.E.S.T.

**MA.5.DP.I.2** | **Math Missions** | **Mode, Median, Range, and Mean in a Data Set**

Roll two number cubes and record the sum on the chart to the left. Do this 15 times total. Then, create a line plot based on the data. Finally, determine the mode, range, median, and mean of your data set.

 + ⚃ = 3

**LINE PLOT**

| Random Number Generator | | |
|---|---|---|
| | | |
| | | |
| | | |
| | | |
| | | |

⟵―――――――――――――――――――――⟶

What is the mode of this set of data?

What is the median of this set of data?

What is the range of this set of data?

What is the mean of this set of data?

# TAKING ON THE B.E.S.T.

## Math Misconception Mystery (PAGE 1)

**BEFORE THE VIDEO:** Solve the problem on your own.

Determine the mode, median, range, and mean for the data set below.

| Terrence's Running Times (in Minutes) | |
|---|---|
| 32 | 45 |
| 33 | 36 |
| 32 | 45 |
| 42 | |

**DURING THE VIDEO:** Pause after each "character" solves the problem and jot down quick notes to help you remember what they did correctly or incorrectly.

Character #1 _____

Character #2 _____

Character #3 _____

Character #4 _____

# TAKING ON THE B.E.S.T.

## Math Misconception Mystery (PAGE 2)

**AFTER THE VIDEO:** Discuss and analyze their answers.

The most reasonable answer belongs to Character # _____ because

_____

_____

_____

_____

(Justify how this character's work makes sense.)

### Let's help the others:

|  | Character #___: | Character #___: | Character #___: |
|---|---|---|---|
| What did this character do that was correct? | | | |
| Identify their error | | | |
| What do they need to know to understand for next time? | | | |